Adobe Photoshop
Elements 5.0

MAXIMUM PERFORMANCE

Unleash the hidden performance of Elements

Mark Galer

ELSEVIER

AMSTERDAM • BOSTON • HEIDELBERG • LONDON • NEW YORK • OXFORD
PARIS • SAN DIEGO • SAN FRANCISCO • SINGAPORE • SYDNEY • TOKYO

Focal Press is an imprint of Elsevier

Focal
Press

Focal Press is an imprint of Elsevier
Linacre House, Jordan Hill, Oxford OX2 8DP, UK
The Boulevard, Langford Lane, Kidlington, Oxford OX5 1GB, UK
84 Theobald's Road, London WC1X 8RR, UK
Radarweg 29, PO Box 211, 1000 AE Amsterdam, The Netherlands
30 Corporate Drive, Suite 400, Burlington, MA 01803, USA
525 B Street, Suite 1900, San Diego, CA 92101-4495, USA

First edition 2007

British Library Cataloguing in Publication Data
A catalogue record for this book is available from the British Library

Library of Congress Cataloguing in Publication Data
A catalogue record for this book is available from the Library of Congress

ISBN–13: 978-0-240-52048-3

ISBN–10: 0-240-52048-3

For more information on all Focal Press publications

visit our website at: www.focalpress.com

Printed and bound in Canada

07 08 09 10 11 11 10 9 8 7 6 5 4 3 2 1

for Dorothy

Picture Credits

Dorothy Connop, www.iStockphoto.com, Jakub Kazmierczak, Daniel Stainsby, Jennifer Stephens, Akane Utsunomiya, Michael Wennrich.

All other images by the author.

Contents - part 1

1

optimize

Contents - part 2

2

enhance

Contents - part 3

3

montage

Contents - dvd

The DVD is a veritable treasure trove of supporting files for the projects in this book as well as a resource for your own creative projects. Just transfer the supporting files to your Photoshop Elements Organizer (see 'Getting Started - page xvii') for fast access to the images and movies. The movies are an invaluable resource allowing you to start, stop and rewind so that the skills can be quickly and easily acquired at your own pace. The DVD also contains multilayered image files (PSDs) of the completed projects, uncompressed TIFF files with saved selections, RAW files and high-quality 16 Bits/Channel files. Loadable presets are also available to enhance your software together with a rich stock library of royalty-free images.

THE DVD PROVIDES EXTENSIVE SUPPORT IN THE FORM OF:

- Over five hours of movie tutorials to guide you through all of the projects in this book. You may need to install the QuickTime movie player from the supporting DVD to watch the movies from the Organizer within Photoshop Elements 5.0.

- High-resolution, high-quality JPEG images to support all of the imaging projects.

- Full-resolution TIFF images with 'saved selections' for users interested in completing the projects in the least amount of time whilst achieving maximum quality.

- Camera RAW and 16 Bits/Channel files.

- 5 high-resolution images courtesty of iStockphoto.com

- Multilayered Photoshop documents (PSD files) of completed projects.

- A stock library of 100 high-resolution, royalty-free images for creative montage work.

- Adobe presets (Layer Styles, Custom Shapes and Gradients) to enhance the performance capabilities of your Adobe Photoshop Elements software.

- Maximum Performance Action files to fast-track your workflows and editing tasks.

- Printable PDF file of keyboard shortcuts to act as a quick and handy reference guide to speed up your image-editing tasks.

- Receive a 10% discount on additional images purchased from iStockphoto.com by quoting the code that is available on the supporting DVD.

Preface

The creative projects in *Adobe Photoshop Elements 5.0 - Maximum Performance* are designed to provide you with the essential techniques for professional quality editing - without the need to upgrade to the full version of Photoshop. The projects are designed to unleash the hidden potential of the budget software through a series of workarounds, advanced techniques and loadable presets. Each creative project is supported by a QuickTime movie tutorial and high-resolution images - all available on a supporting DVD. The DVD contains full and comprehensive movie support together with a library of royalty-free, high-resolution stock images for self-initiated creative projects. Each project is designed to build the skills required so that any photographer can attain the status of 'imaging guru'. The magic is deconstructed using a series of easy to follow step-by-step projects using large clear screen grabs and jargon-free explanations. Completed multilayered project files are also available on the DVD for those users who like to have access to the completed project for comparison and analysis.

This book will act as your guide to some of Elements' less well-known and more powerful post-production editing techniques. It will enable you to attain the same high-quality images as professionals using the full version of Photoshop. This book makes Elements a viable alternative to the full version of Photoshop for imaging professionals and enthusiasts looking to extract the maximum performance from their software.

This book is primarily concerned with the post-production stage of the creative process and demonstrates how this part of the creative process can optimize and enhance the original capture or create an entirely new image out of several images (the creation of a composite photograph or photomontage). Where appropriate the book will discuss measures that can be taken by the photographer in pre-production or production to enable the highest-quality outcome as a result of the post-production stage. To ensure the best quality image from our sophisticated and professional post-production techniques we should ensure that we access quality raw materials whenever possible - 'quality in, quality out'. The vast majority of the JPEG images on the supporting DVD were processed from either camera RAW files or high-quality 16 Bits/Channel scans. Most of the images featured in this book were captured using budget digital SLR and fixed lens digital cameras such as the Fuji FinePix s7000, s9000 and Olympus E300, affordable cameras used to capture information-rich images.

The techniques used in this book promote a non-destructive approach to image editing wherever possible. The term 'non-destructive image editing' refers to the process of editing an image whilst retaining as much of the original information as possible and editing in such a way that any modifications can be usually undone or modified. Editing on the base layer of the image can often mean that modifications to the pixel information cannot be undone easily or at all, e.g. sharpening an image file cannot be undone once the file has been saved and flattened. It is however possible to sharpen non-destructively in post-production so that the amount of sharpening can be altered when the file is opened at a later date. This latter approach would be termed 'non-destructive'. When capturing images with a digital camera many users do not realize that if the JPEG file format is used image processing starts in the camera. Color correction, contrast adjustment, saturation levels and sharpening all take place in the camera. If maximum quality is to be realized the RAW format should be chosen in preference to the JPEG format, if possible. The post-production decisions can then be left to the Adobe software, allowing the user many more options.

Photoshop Elements replaced 'Photoshop LE' (limited edition - as in limited function and not availability); both of these software packages share something in common - they offer limited elements of the full version of Photoshop. Adobe strips out some of the features that would be the first port of call for some professional image editors and photographers, but this does not mean that the same level of control cannot be achieved when using the budget software. Professional post-production image editing does NOT have to be compromised by using Photoshop Elements. With editing images there is usually more than a single way to reach the destination or required outcome. With a good roadmap the Elements user can reach the same destination by taking a slightly different course. These roads are often poorly signposted, so are often inaccessible to the casual user of the software. This book will act as your guide to enable you to attain a broad range of sophisticated post-production image-editing skills through a series of creative projects designed to circumnavigate the missing features.

Photoshop Elements IS a viable alternative to the full version of Photoshop for most professional image-editing tasks. Many professionals may disagree with this statement, as a quick glance at the Elements package may result in a long list of the elements that are missing rather than taking a long hard look at the elements that remain (a case of 'the glass is half-empty' rather than 'the glass is half-full'). After a decade of professional image editing I have learnt that there is more than one way to create an image. There is no 'one way'. In short, it is possible to take a high-quality image file and work non-destructively to create an image which is indistinguishable from one that has been optimized using the full version of Photoshop. This book does not aim to outline every tool in your kit (a paintbrush doesn't really require an owner's manual and some of the automated features are sometimes more trouble than they are worth). It just deals with how to adapt the tools you do have to perform the tasks you didn't think you were able to. It aims to show you that Elements is better equipped than you were led to believe. Photoshop Elements really is the proverbial wolf in sheep's clothes.

mark galer

Location Image by Dorothy Connop

Getting Started

Most users of this book will have some experience of digital imaging and Photoshop Elements, but just check the following to make sure all is in order before you start.

Following orders

The commands in Photoshop Elements allow the user to modify digital files and are accessed via menus and submenus. The commands used in the projects are listed as a hierarchy, with the main menu indicated first and the submenu or command second, e.g. Main menu > Command. For example, the command for applying a Levels adjustment would be indicated as follows: Enhance > Adjust Lighting > Levels. If you get stuck or are unclear watch the movie on the supporting DVD and follow my mouse cursor to help you find what you are looking for.

Calibrate your monitor

If your images are going to look good everywhere - not just on your own monitor - it is advised that you calibrate your monitor (set the optimum color, brightness and contrast). If you don't have access to a monitor calibration device I would recommend that you take a look at Adobe Gamma in the 'Control Panel' of your PC. I would recommend that you use a 'Hardware White Point' or 'Color Temperature' of '6500° K (daylight)'.

Note > If using Adobe Gamma on an LCD monitor ignore the recommendation to turn up the monitor contrast.

Color Settings

The colors are kept consistent between devices such as cameras, computers and printers through the use of color profiles. If you intend to print your images you would be advised to go to Edit > Color Settings and then click on the radio button that says 'Always Optimize for Printing'. Elements will now use the larger Adobe RGB profile instead of the smaller sRGB profile.

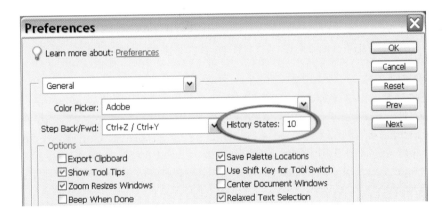

Memory

You will be working on images in excess of 5 megapixels (the supporting DVD provides high-resolution images for ALL of the creative projects in this book). This professional level of image editing can place a strain on a computer's working memory or RAM. It is advised that you install at least 512 MB of RAM (1 gigabyte or more is not considered excessive when editing very large image files) so that the image editing you are about to undertake does not begin to crawl. Shut down any other applications that you are not using so that all of the available memory is made available to Photoshop Elements. Photoshop Elements keeps a memory of your image-editing process, which it calls the 'History States'. The default setting in the General Preferences (Edit > Preferences > General) is 50 History States. Allowing the user to track back 50 commands, or clicks of the mouse, can again place an enormous strain on the working memory. I would recommend that you lower this figure to 10 for most editing work. This can be readjusted without restarting the software should you wish to increase Photoshop's memory for your editing actions. Just remember that the more memory you dedicate to what you have just done, the less you have available for what you are about to do. Also in Preferences > Memory and Image Cache check that the lion's share of your RAM is dedicated to Photoshop Elements (at least 85%). Photoshop Elements will also be using your 'scratch disk' or 'hard drive' in the image-editing process so be sure to keep plenty of gigabytes of free space available.

Give yourself some elbow room

I recommend that you keep the 'Photo Bin' and 'Palette Bin' closed until you need them (go to Window > Palette Bin). This will maximize the area on your screen for viewing the image you are editing. Only the Layers palette is used all of the time in advanced image editing. In the default mode it is stacked with the other palettes in the Palette Bin. Locate the Layers palette and drag it out into the working area before closing the Bins. Similarly the Tools palette on the left side of the screen can be dragged to new locations so that it can be close to the action. I prefer to view the image in a window rather than in 'Maximize' mode. This allows me to see the additional information that is displayed in the title bar together with the magnification. I like to view my images at 50% or 100% (actual pixels) to gain a more accurate idea of the image quality. This information is also available in the Navigator palette but, as I use 'keyboard shortcuts' for moving and zooming in and out of images, I usually keep this palette closed as well.

Keyboard shortcuts

Many commands that can be accessed via the menus and submenus can also be accessed via keyboard shortcuts. A shortcut is the action of pressing keys on the keyboard to carry out a command (rather than clicking a command or option in a menu). Shortcuts speed up digital image processing enormously and it is worth learning the examples given in the study guides. If in doubt use the menu (the shortcut will be indicated next to the command) until you become more familiar with the key combinations. See the 'Keyboard shortcuts' section at the end of the book for a list of the most frequently used shortcuts.

Note > Macintosh owners should use the Command instead of the Ctrl key.

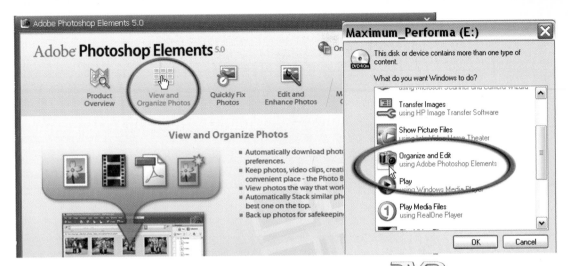

Accessing the support images and movies

Open the Organizer from the Photoshop Elements welcome screen or click on the Organize icon directly above the Options bar in the Edit workspace. Install the DVD and click on the 'Organize and Edit' option if asked. Alternatively click on the Get Photos icon in the Organizer workspace (the little camera) and choose the 'From Files and Folders' option. Then locate the DVD (My Computer > Maximum Performance) and the resource folder you want to import. The JPEG files are high quality and will not take up much space on your hard drive. The TIFF files take up a little more room on your hard drive but have the advantage of containing 'saved selections' that can be used to speed up the completion of the projects.

IMPORTANT: You may need to install the latest version of the QuickTime movie player that is available on the DVD before watching the movies in the Organizer workspace. Movies are recorded using both Elements 4.0 and Elements 5.0 software. Where Elements 4.0 software has been used all commands and procedures remain the same.

Deselect the 'Automatically Fix Red Eyes' option and then click on the Get Photos button. Your images or movies will be imported and organized. Click on the 'Import Batch' option in the bottom left-hand corner of the organizer window to see the images as a collection. Use the keyboard shortcut Ctrl+I to open any image in the Editor workspace. Double-click on any Movie icon to watch the movie within the Organizer workspace.

Maximum Performance actions

On the DVD is a folder titled E5MP_Actions. These are a series of files that I have prepared that will enable you to perform a series of automated editing procedures for fast-tracking some of the skills presented in this book - a single click of the mouse that instructs Photoshop Elements to conduct an automated series of steps in just a few seconds. These actions may complete the editing task or just fast-track some of the repetitive editing procedures to get you further along the editing process with the minimum of fuss. The Maximum Performance actions folder on the DVD should be placed in the Photo Creations folder that Elements 5.0 uses to access its various templates, layer styles and special effects. Once the folder is placed into the correct location your Photoshop Elements software should be restarted before it can access these performance features.

When you see the Maximum Performance Action logo in Part 2 and Part 3 of this book certain steps can be fast-tracked with just a few clicks of your mouse.

Loading the Maximum Performance actions

Although the Photo Creations folder is buried deep in the C: drive of your computer the procedure must only be completed once. Simply access the C: drive of your computer and look for the Documents and Settings folder. Then proceed to All Users (All Users.Windows) > Application Data > Adobe > Photoshop Elements > 5.0 > Photo Creations. The illustration above shows you the precise location of the folder on my computer. Then drag the E5MP_Actions folder into this location. Restart the Photoshop Elements software and wait a couple of minutes whilst Photoshop rebuilds its 'Artwork and Effects' database.

Using the actions

The actions can be accessed through the Artwork and Effects palette. Click on the Special Effects icon in this palette and choose E5MP_actions from the menu. Click on an action and then simply hit the Apply button. Some of the actions may require opacity changes in the layers to fine-tune the effect or some further work as in the case of the Dodge and Burn action. Try combining various actions to create different effects.

Note > The masking actions are intended for the montage projects outlined in Part 3 of this book and will only work when a second layer named Layer 1 is sitting above the background layer.

iStock_000001683436 Headshot by aldra

MAXIMUM PERFORMANCE ACTIONS

This stock image (courtesy of www.iStockphoto.com) was created using multiple actions. The soft focus effect was first applied and then followed by the Vignette, Dodge and Burn, Split Tone and Sharpen actions. A Transform command was used on the vignette and a little painting in the Dodge and Burn layer was needed to brighten the teeth and eyes in this 3-minute makeover.

part 1

optimize

Project 1

Crop and Correct

This simple project will unmask some of the hidden features of the Straighten and Crop tools enabling you to optimize your images for print or screen viewing. You will learn that you can straighten, resize and crop your image with just a few clicks, and that the Free Transform command can correct any unnatural perspective resulting from using wide angle lenses. Quality starts here.

Ensure the horizon lines of your images do not resemble ski slopes by making use of the fabulous new Straighten tool

1. Open the image from the supporting DVD in the Standard Edit workspace. Click on the 'Straighten tool' in the Tools palette. Select the option 'Grow Canvas to Fit' in the Options bar above the image window. Now click on the horizon line and, with the mouse clicker held down, drag a line along the horizon line of the image. The image will automatically be straightened.

2. When we size an image we should select the width and height in pixels for screen or web viewing, and in centimeters or inches for printing. Typing in 'px', 'in' or 'cm' after each measurement will tell Elements to crop using these units. If no measurement is entered in the field then Photoshop Elements will choose the default unit measurement entered in the preferences (Preferences > Units & Rulers). The preference can be quickly changed by right-clicking on either ruler (select 'View > Rulers' if they are not currently selected).

3. The action of entering measurements and a resolution at the time of cropping ensures that the image is sized (pixel dimensions altered) and cropped (shaped) in one action. Entering the size at the time of cropping ensures the aspect ratio of the final image will match the printing paper, photo frame or screen where the image will finally be output.

Note > If an aspect ratio or both width and height measurements are entered into the measurement fields, the proportions of the final crop will be locked. This new aspect ratio may differ from that of the original capture and this in turn may prevent you from selecting either the full width or full height of the image, e.g. if you have entered the same measurement in both the width and height fields the final crop proportions are constrained to a square.

PERFORMANCE TIP

If you need to crop to an aspect ratio (such as a widescreen 16:9 TV aspect ratio), but do not wish to shed excess pixels from the image file, then leave the 'Resolution field' in the Options bar blank. You also have the option of choosing an alternate shield color when cropping images by going to 'Edit > Preferences > Display and Cursors > Crop Tool'.

5

4. Drag the cropping marquee over the image to create the best composition. Drag any of the corner handles, or click and drag inside the crop marquee, to adjust the composition and then commit the crop by clicking on the tick or double-clicking inside the crop marquee. The image should get smaller on the screen as excess pixels are discarded. If the image grows on screen Photoshop Elements is adding pixels (upsampling), which can lead to a loss of quality. If this happens you need to either start with a larger image file or decrease the output dimensions. It is important to save this cropped version using a different name to ensure the higher resolution master file is preserved.

PERFORMANCE TIP

When using the Straighten tool to align to a vertical within the image you must hold down the Ctrl key whilst dragging your line to prevent the image from being rotated to the horizontal format.

The Straighten tool is disabled for 16 Bits/Channel images. To straighten an image without the Straighten tool first move the edge of the crop marquee to either a vertical or horizontal line within the image. Move the cursor to a position just outside one of the corner handles of the cropping marquee and when the double-headed curved arrow appears you can rotate the cropping marquee to align it with the horizontal or vertical within the image. Then extend the cropping marquee by dragging one of the corner handles.

IMAGE ON DVD

Correct Camera Distortion

When a camera is tilted up or down with a short focal length lens (wide angle) the verticals within the image can lean excessively inwards or outwards (converging verticals). Professional architectural photographers use cameras with movements or special lenses to remove this excessive distortion. To correct the perspective with Elements 5.0 use the new Correct Camera Distortion filter.

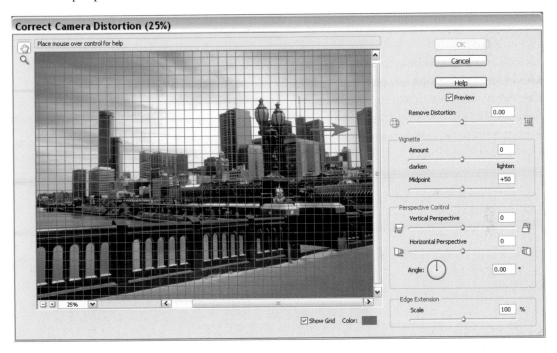

1. You may choose to duplicate the background layer by dragging it to the Create a New Layer icon in the Layers palette before you start the process. Select the duplicate layer in the Layers palette and then select the Correct Camera Distortion filter from the Filters menu. The grid should be on by default and you can change its color if it's not clear against the subject you are viewing. The top slider in this dialog box corrects either barrel distortion or pincushion distortion, which sometimes results when using the extreme focal lengths of the zoom lens. Both result in curved straight lines which are usually most noticeable with the curvature of a horizon line when using a short focal length lens (wide angle).

2. Drag the Vertical Perspective slider in the Perspective Control section of the dialog box to render all the vertical lines in the image parallel. Use the grid lines to align the verticals within the image. Use the keyboard shortcuts to access the Zoom tool (Control+Spacebar and Alt+Spacebar) if you need to zoom in on a vertical to check the accuracy of the correction. You may need to alter the angle to ensure absolute accuracy.

PERFORMANCE TIP

As the corrected image is narrower on one or more edges after using the Remove Distortion or Perspective Correction sliders you can use the Edge Extension slider at the bottom of the dialog box so that the corrected image fills the image window. As this process involves Photoshop adding pixels to grow the image some users may choose to crop the image instead of scaling the image in this dialog box.

3. The Correct Camera Distortion filter also has control over vignetting. Vignettes are often used for creative reasons to fade an image to black or white at the edges and corners. Some wide angle lenses, vignette when used at very wide apertures and these effects can be reduced or removed using the sliders in the Correct Camera Distortion dialog box. In the example image above a value of +35 is used to remove the darkened corners of the image that resulted from using a wide angle lens. The midpoint slider should be used to control the width of the correction, i.e. raising the value of the midpoint slider will restrict the lightening effect to just the extreme outer regions of the image window whilst lowering the value will broaden the lightening effect. In later projects the Correct Camera Distortion filter can be used to creatively darken the corners of images to increase the sense of drama and mood.

This project demonstrates how the Straighten, Crop and Correct Camera Distortion tools can be used to size and shape your images so that they appear tailor-made every time.

Project 2

Levels

This project will guide the user safely through the tricky mountain passes of the primary and essential technique used to achieve quality digital images. The adjustment feature is called 'Levels', but when you are presented with the virtual mountain range on opening the Levels dialog box, you begin to wonder what the clever people at Adobe were thinking of when they gave this indispensable adjustment feature its wonderful name (I think it's called irony).

16 BITS/CHANNEL
IMAGE ON DVD

Levels - optimized quality starts here

1. In the illustration above one might be forgiven for thinking that the black peaks in the dialog box are an indication of how high the mountains are in the image, but no, it is really an indicator of how many pixels of each tone are present in the image. If the image is dark then the mountains will be higher on the left side. If the image is very light, the mountains will be taller on the right side. The first step in nearly all image-editing tasks is the need to optimize the tonality or 'dynamic range' of the image by adjusting the 'Levels'.

Finding your levels > In Elements go to the Enhance menu and select 'Levels' from the Adjust Lighting submenu.

If you are a newcomer to this dialog box you may simply want to click on the Auto button and then click OK. This simple procedure ensures the tonality of the digital image starts with a deep black and finishes with a bright white for optimum contrast and visual impact. If you want to perform the task manually click on the black slider underneath the mountain range (the triangle on the left) and drag it to where the mountains start. If you are now looking for the little triangle at the foot of the photographic mountains instead of the virtual ones, then I suggest you go and lie down for a moment and come back refreshed. Do the same with the white slider on the right and you are almost finished. Click and drag the gray slider in the middle to make the image brighter or darker (depending on which way you drag the slider). If you want to start impressing the neighbors then you may like to start calling the gray triangle the 'Gamma slider'.

Warning > You should avoid using the destructive Brightness/Contrast adjustment from the same submenu as the image will often look far from enhanced if used.

2. If you drag the sliders too far you will lose or 'clip' information from the image file. Shadows will become black and highlights will become white. Your detail will have sunk without a trace into the black holes of our virtual valleys (called 'level 0') or have been pushed off the top of the virtual peaks (called 'level 255'). If you fear the numbers 0 and 255 (which every self-respecting photographer should) you could try the following top tip. Hold down the Alt key and drag the Shadow or Highlight slider towards the mountains (your image will disappear momentarily but fear not). Colors will start to appear in your main image window when information is being lost. Move the sliders back until these colors disappear. If colors are still appearing in the image window with the sliders all the way back to the edge of the histogram then your image was either underexposed or overexposed in your camera. If you are really unlucky you will have lost detail both in the shadows and in the highlights as a result of the photographers worst enemy - excessive contrast. Not even the magic called Photoshop Elements can dig you out of this hole, my friend, if you failed to 'bracket' your exposures.

3. Users who have acquired images at a higher bit depth using camera RAW or a scanner set to 48-bit scanning should now drop their images to 8 Bits/Channel (Image > Mode > 8 Bits/Channel). The secret to intelligent color adjustment is that the grass may 'really' be greener on the other side. Until you have seen the other side how will you know? With this in mind Adobe has given us 'Color Variations'. It is a simple case of 'if you see something else you like - you can have it'.

16-bit editing

16-bit editing has been a reality for Elements users since version 3.0. If you have acquired your image from the Camera RAW dialog box or a 48-bit scanner then you will need to drop the bit depth to 8 bits to complete the following steps because although Elements supports 16-bit editing it does not support the use of adjustment layers with which to edit the bit-rich pictures. Adjusting the levels of your image in 16 bits per channel and then dropping to the more time-efficient 8 bits per channel mode keeps you on the path to maximum quality.

4. From the Enhance menu choose 'Variations' from the Adjust Color menu. Yes, I know it's a big box. It needs to be this size so they can get all of the lovely colors in. Just follow the numbers in the box. Start by selecting the Midtones radio button and then adjust the intensity until you can see the flavoured thumbnails look about right (not too loud please), and then click on the one you like (color blind males may need a woman's touch just about now). Then click OK. For those who have found bliss you can stop this project now - or for those who still want to take another look at that grass, press on to step 5.

Warning > Clicking on anything other than 'Midtones' in this dialog box may be harmful to the health of your pixels that you so lovingly looked after in the Levels dialog box.

$5.$ We have just completed our global adjustments (all of the pixels in the image have changed in brightness and color). We will now set about changing just a select few. To isolate pixels for a 'localized adjustment' we have to select them with (yes - you guessed it) a 'selection tool'. We will start with the very wobbly Lasso tool (there are three in the stack so make sure you get the right one - click, and hold your clicker down, on the little black arrow in the corner of the Lasso tool to see your options). Now draw (yes I know drawing isn't everybody's strong point) along the terraced fields in the foreground of the image (don't let go of the mouse clicker - not even when you get to the end of the field) and then circle (what else would you expect to do with a lasso?) beneath the image and around until you get back to the point where you started - now let go. Those things that have appeared are called 'marching ants'. Don't worry about how wobbly your drawing is at this stage.

Note > If you did happen to let go (even though I told you not to) before you had finished the selection, go to the Select menu, choose 'Deselect', and then start again (this time paying closer attention to not letting go of your clicker).

Now if your drawing (like mine) leaves a lot to be desired, we can fix it up by painting it better in the next step (my painting isn't much better than my drawing either, but at least with the brush we can let go of the clicker without unleashing the mad ants and take a breather for a while).

PERFORMANCE TIP

Elements users do not have a Quick Mask mode that is found in the full version of Photoshop. They must use the Selection Brush tool to fix up the very disturbing attempts with the lasso or the not-so-magic Magic Wand tool. The Selection Brush tool icon in the Tools palette has a circle of ants emanating from the tip of the brush (wow - a brush that paints ants - how wonderful). Now painting ants is too weird for me so I usually choose 'Mask' from the Mode menu in the Options bar (positioned above the image window) to replicate the Quick Mask mode found in the full version of Photoshop.

6. Choose the 'Selection Brush tool' and the 'Mask' option in the Options bar. Set the brush hardness to 100% and start painting your mask better. If your paint has strayed over the line, you will need to hold down the Alt key and paint to remove the paint (strange but true). Take your time - no rush - zoom in if you can't see what you are doing and paint on the bigger picture.

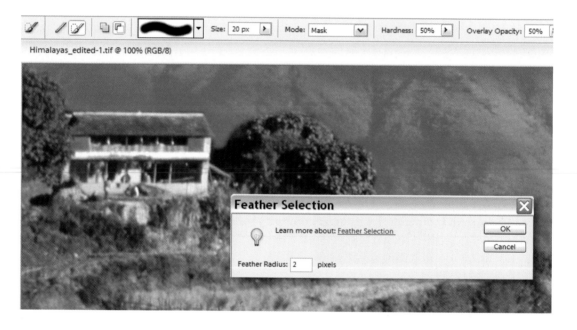

7. Just trust me on the next step OK. I want you to 'feather your selection'. Choose 'Feather' from the Select menu and then enter a value of 2 in the 'Feather Radius' field.

When you click OK watch the edge of your brushwork - it goes sort of soft. If you missed it go to the Edit menu and choose 'Undo' and then 'Redo'. Zoom in if you still didn't see it change. I need you to see it change so you don't think I am messing with your head on this one. So why is soft better than hard you ask? Soft is good (in this instance) because it is hard to pick a soft transition between pixels that have been adjusted and those that missed the boat, i.e. no one will be able to tell that you have been 'tweaking' (aka enhancing) your image. At the moment however you have not tweaked anything, merely isolated it for tweaking.

Note > If the terminology 'Feather Selection', when you are in fact looking at a mask, is troubling you then you have my permission to select 'Selection' in the Options bar instead of 'Mask' before feathering. The advantage to feathering or blurring the selection, when it is being viewed as a mask, is that you can see whether the amount of feather is appropriate, and adjust the pixel radius according to the softness of the edge that looks right for your image. Bigger images (more megapixels) require more feathering as a rule.

TIFF IMAGE WITH SAVED
SELECTION ON DVD

Warning > Too much feathering is as bad as none at all, i.e. now the color corrections will bleed into the adjacent image and make it look like your colors are running.

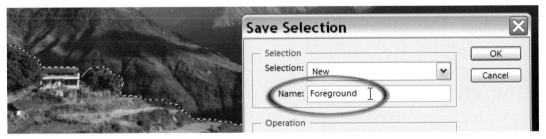

8. Because making a selection can be the most time-consuming part of the process, and because computers crash (no really they do), Adobe allows you to save your artwork (the selection). Go to the Select menu and choose 'Save Selection' - give it a name, choose OK and then save your image file by going to the File menu and choosing 'Save As'. This will allow you to choose a different name and save it as a different file to the one you originally opened. In this way you will have one original and one enhanced/stuffed file just for good measure. You can now lie down for five minutes to rest the gray matter and then return to your enhanced/stuffed file - go to the Select menu and choose 'Load Selection'.

9. With the marching ants running rampant all around your selected pixels I now want you to find the Layers palette. If it is hiding then you can summon it up from the depths of oblivion by going to the Window menu and selecting - yes you guessed it again - 'Layers'. Click on the little round icon that is half black and half white. Click on the icon and choose 'Levels' from this submenu.

10. Now a couple of really interesting things have happened (well mildly interesting for a computer geek anyway). First, and not surprisingly, the virtual mountains have reappeared - but this time they represent only the selected pixels and not the pixels of the entire image (hence the different shape). Second, the ants have mysteriously disappeared, only to be replaced by a new layer in the Layers palette. This layer is called an 'adjustment layer' and it will play host to the adjustments we are about to make in this Levels dialog box. Third, the mask has reappeared in a little thumbnail image to the right of the Adjustment icon in the Layers palette. This is called a 'layer mask' and it will hide any adjustments we make in the unselected portion of the image (the distant mountains and sky).

Move the Highlight slider (the white triangle on the right) in towards the slopes of the histogram and move the central gray triangle (the Gamma slider) to the left to brighten the selected pixels.

Note > The Adjustment Layer icon changes with the preferences set for this palette - so don't worry if yours doesn't look the same as mine.

PERFORMANCE TIP

Now we could have picked up the Levels command from the Enhance menu, as in step 1 of this very exciting project. The difference is that adjustments made using an adjustment layer are infinitely editable. Infinite editing is great for people who are indecisive about color, want to make frequent changes and don't want to degrade the quality of their image by doing so. The changes you make when you use an adjustment layer are not actually applied to the pixels at this point. The adjustment layer acts like a filter showing us a view of how the pixels will look when the adjustments are applied. If you make frequent changes to the actual pixels themselves you will eventually degrade the image quality. Using adjustment layers you can make changes till the cows come home and never degrade the quality of the image. Your adjustments are only applied once - when your editing is complete and your image is either saved for screen viewing or printed.

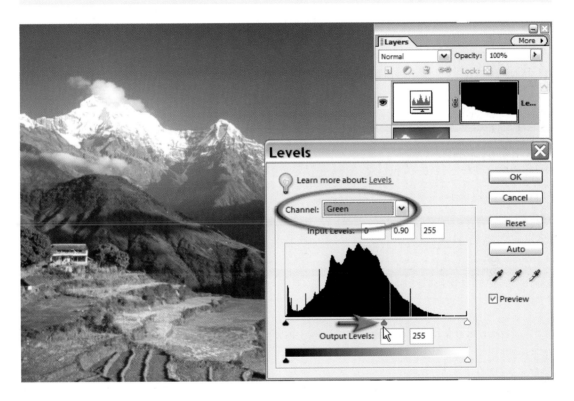

11. Because the grass is sometimes too green on the other side we can go to the 'Green' channel in the Channel menu, positioned near the top of the Levels dialog box, and move the gray triangle to the right. This will make the grass less green. These adjustments will have the effect of making the foreground look sunnier (brighter, more contrasty and warmer usually does the trick). Select OK and sit back and admire a job well done. Zoom in to look for bleeding color or areas that should have been in the selection that were left out.

12. If you have found any errors they can usually be attributed to the mask. To work on the mask you can click on its thumbnail in the Layers palette and paint with either white or black. This time you will need to select the real paintbrush and not the one that paints ants. Pressing the letter D on the keyboard will make sure the colors in the Tools palette are set to their default settings of white and black. Black will remove the adjustments and white will allow the adjustments to affect the pixels below. Use a slightly soft brush to match the softening you have done to your mask. If you want to see the mask during this operation you will need to hold down the Alt and the Shift keys at the same time whilst clicking on the layer mask thumbnail. Repeat this action to return to the normal view.

13. Don't forget the final step of any editing procedure is the Unsharp Mask. I always prefer to create a separate layer for the sharpening process - especially if I am intending to make a print. My procedure is to choose 'Select All' from the Select menu, 'Copy Merged' and then 'Paste', both from the Edit menu. Set the view to 'Actual Pixels' from the View menu before going to the Filter menu to choose the 'Unsharp Mask' option from the Sharpen submenu. Standard settings are around 100% for the amount, 1.5 for the Radius when sharpening a 5 or 6 megapixel image with a threshold of around 3, or slightly more if your image is slightly noisy or has already been sharpened in-camera.

A print has a habit of looking less sharp than the screen image so a little bit of oversharpening is usually required to get things looking perfect. If you can't see any sharpening then you need to check that you do not have the adjustment layer selected. You cannot sharpen invisible pixels, i.e. there are no pixels on an adjustment layer to be sharpened. Project 5 will look at advanced skills for sharpening localized areas of the image.

PERFORMANCE TIP
If this sharpening layer is beneath the adjustment layer, the adjustments will be applied twice, and then your image will look like it has had a tussle with the ugly stick. If this happens you should drag the new layer to the top of the layers stack. Remember that when you choose 'Paste' from the Edit menu the pixels are always pasted into a new layer above the active layer.

Project 3

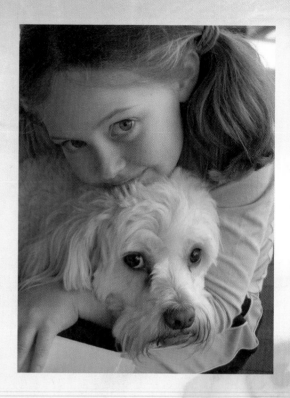

Camera RAW

All digital cameras capture in RAW but only digital SLRs and the medium to high end 'prosumer' cameras offer the user the option of saving the images in this RAW format. Selecting the RAW format in the camera instead of JPEG or TIFF stops the camera from processing the color data collected from the sensor. Digital cameras typically process the data collected by the sensor by applying the white balance, sharpening and contrast settings set by the user in the camera's menus. The camera then compresses the bit depth of the color data from 12 to 8 bits per channel before saving the file as a JPEG or TIFF file. Selecting the RAW format prevents this image processing taking place. The RAW data is what the sensor 'saw' before the camera processed the image, and many photographers have started to refer to this file as the 'digital negative'. This digital negative allows you to take control over the conversion process to access maximum quality.

RAW IMAGE ON DVD

For maximum quality choose to save your files using the camera RAW format. This image was further edited in the main editing workspace using techniques from the Hue and Saturation and Glamor Portrait projects

Processing RAW data

White balance, brightness, contrast, saturation and sharpness can all be assigned as part of the conversion process in Adobe camera RAW rather than in the camera. Performing these image-editing tasks on the full high-bit RAW data enables you to achieve a higher quality end result. After the image has been processed in the camera RAW dialog box the file is then opened into the image-editing workspace and the RAW file closes and remains in its RAW state, i.e. unaffected by the processing procedure. Although the camera RAW dialog box appears a little daunting at first sight, it is reasonably intuitive and easy to master.

1. Open the RAW file from the supporting DVD. Set the white balance by choosing one of the presets from the drop-down menu. If none of the presets adjusts the color to your satisfaction you can manually adjust the Temperature and Tint sliders to remove any color cast present. The Temperature slider controls the blue/yellow color balance whilst the Tint slider controls the green/magenta balance. Moving both the sliders in the same direction controls the red/cyan balance. Alternatively you can simply click on the White Balance eyedropper in the small tools palette (top left-hand corner of the dialog box) and then click on any neutral tone you can find in the image. In this image click on the white paper the girl is holding.

Note > Although it is a 'White Balance' you actually need to click on a tone that is not too bright. Clicking on a light or mid gray is preferable. A photographer looking to save a little time later may introduce a 'gray card' in the first frame of a shoot to simplify this task.

2. Set the tonal range of the image using the Exposure, Shadows and Brightness sliders. These sliders behave like the input sliders in the Levels dialog box and will set the black and white points within the image. The Brightness slider adjusts the midtone values in a similar way to the Gamma slider when using Levels dialog. When tall peaks appear at either end of the histogram you will lose shadow, highlight or color detail when you export the file to the main editing software. Careful adjustment of these sliders will allow you to get the best out of the dynamic range of your imaging sensor, thereby creating a tonally rich image with full detail.

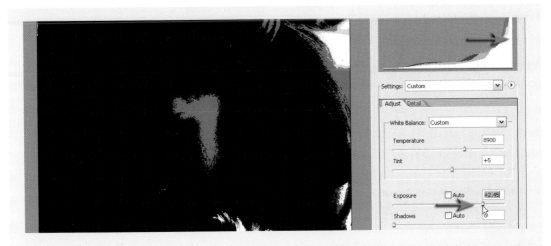

PERFORMANCE TIP

Hold down the Alt key when adjusting either the Exposure or Shadows slider to view the point at which highlight or shadow clipping begins to occur (the point at which pixels lose detail in one or more channels). Alternatively you can check the Shadows and Highlights boxes above the main image window instead of holding down the Alt key.

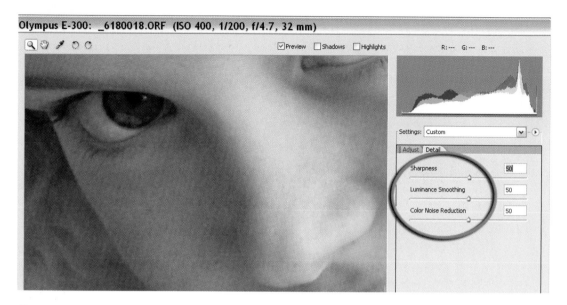

3. Set the image to 100% and click on the Detail tab to access the sharpness and noise reduction controls. The Luminance Smoothing and Color Noise Reduction sliders (designed to tackle the camera noise that occurs when the image sensors' ISO is high) should only be raised from 0 if you notice image artifacts such as noise appearing in the image window.

In the project image the sensor was set to 400 ISO on a budget DSLR. Both luminance and color noise are evident when the image is set to 100%. With more expensive DSLR cameras set to 100 ISO it is common to leave all three sliders set to 0. It is recommended that you only perform a gentle amount of sharpening in the RAW dialog box if you intend to selectively sharpen the image in the main image-editing workspace (see 'Project 7 - Sharpening' for localized sharpening techniques that are unavailable in the camera RAW dialog box).

PERFORMANCE TIP
The Luminance Smoothing and Color Noise Reduction sliders can remove subtle detail and color information that may go unnoticed if the photographer is not careful to pay attention to the effects of these sliders. Zoom in to take a closer look and unless you can see either little white speckles or color artifacts set these sliders to 0.

4. The only step that remains is to select the 'Depth' in the lower left-hand corner of the dialog box and then click OK. If the user selects the '16 Bits/Channel' option, the 12 bits per channel data from the image sensor is rounded up – each channel is now capable of supporting 32, 769 levels instead of 256. Many of the advanced editing features are unavailable in 16 Bits/Channel mode so the user may choose to elect for the '8 Bits/Channel' option now. This is OK so long as the tonality (black and white points) and color have been corrected in the camera RAW dialog box.

If the color and tonal information is edited significantly in the main editing space, with the files in 8 Bits/Channel mode, the final quality will be compromised. If the digital image has been corrected sufficiently for the requirements of the output device in the RAW dialog box the file can be edited in 8-bit mode with no apparent loss in quality.

PERFORMANCE TIP

Adobe has created a universal RAW file format called 'DNG' (Digital Negative) in an attempt to ensure that all camera RAW files (whichever camera they originate from) will be accessible in the future. The 'Save' option in the camera RAW dialog box gives you access to convert your camera's RAW file to the Adobe Digital Negative format with no loss of quality. The conversion will ensure that your files are archived in a format that will be understood in the future. Expect to see future models of many digital cameras using this DNG format as standard. One thing is for sure - RAW files are a valuable source of the rich visual data that many of us value, and so the format will be around for many years to come.

Project 4

Target Tones

Setting the levels in a digital image is only the first step to achieving optimized images. It is also necessary to optimize the image for the intended output device. To achieve optimum tonal quality in your digital images it is important to target both the highlight and shadow tones within each image. When using Elements the Eyedropper tool is a key to unlocking the quality that lies dormant in any one of your images which has been correctly exposed.

DVD

16 BITS/CHANNEL
IMAGE ON DVD

What you see is not what you always get - target your levels to your output device for predictable results

To achieve maximum quality set the target levels in images that are in 16 Bits/Channel mode (accessed through the camera RAW format or via scans from film that have been requested as 48-bit output scans). If you are optimizing your files in 8 Bits/Channel mode (via JPEG files) be sure to use an adjustment layer rather than an adjustment from the Enhance menu.

Ansel Adams was responsible for creating the famous/infamous 'Zone System' in order to precisely control the tonal range of each of his masterpieces. If you look carefully at one of his beautiful landscape photographs you will notice that only the light source (or its reflection - something termed a 'specular highlight') appears as paper white. All the rest of the bright highlights reveal tone or texture. Likewise, the shadows may appear very dark, but they are not devoid of detail. Ansel was careful only to render black holes as black. Any surface, even those in shadow, would render glorious amounts of subtle detail.

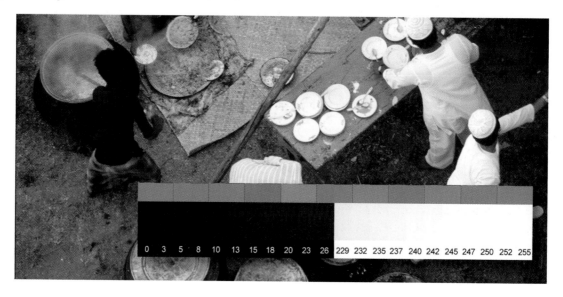

Even though you have set your levels (as guided in Project 2 or 3) it is no guarantee that your highlight or shadow tones will be visible in the final print. To make sure the highlight detail does not 'blow out' (become white) and the shadow detail is not lost in a sea of black ink it is possible to target or set specific tonal values to these important tones. The tones that should be targeted are the lightest and darkest areas in the image that contain detail. The default settings of the eyedroppers to be found in the Levels dialog box are set to 0 (black) and 255 (white). These settings are only useful for targeting the white overexposed areas or black underexposed areas. These tools can however be recalibrated to something much more useful, i.e. tones with detail. A typical photo quality inkjet printer printing on premium grade photo paper will usually render detail between the levels 15 and 250. Precise values can be gained by printing a 'step wedge' of specific tones to evaluate the darkest tone that is not black and the brightest tone that is not paper white (see 'Project 8 - Printing' for more guidance on this subject).

PERFORMANCE TIP

The precise target values for images destined for the commercial printing industry are dependent on the inks, papers and processes in use. Images are sometimes optimized for press by skilled operatives during the conversion to CMYK. Sometimes they are not. If in doubt you should check with the publication to get an idea of what you are expected to do and what you should be aiming for if the responsibility is yours.

1. For maximum quality you would be wise to optimize your histogram in camera RAW or in 16 Bits/Channel mode. If the file is in 16 Bits/Channel mode you will need to access a levels adjustment from the Enhance > Adjust Lighting submenu. If the file is in 8 Bits/Channel mode (due to being captured using the JPEG file format you are advised to create a levels adjustment layer by clicking on the Create New Fill or Adjustment Layer icon in the Layers palette. A tall peak at either level 0 or level 255 is a strong indicator that detail has already been lost either by excessive subject contrast or inappropriate exposure during the capture stage. If this is the case your shadow or highlight detail is already irrecoverable.

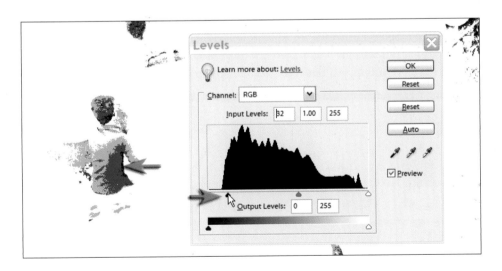

2. Hold down the Alt key and drag the Shadow slider to the right. Keep dragging the slider until the darkest shadows become visible in the image window. Carefully view the image to locate the darkest shadow or surface within the image. Be careful to make a mental note of the position of a representative tone, e.g. a dark surface rather than a black hole and then return the Shadow slider to level 0.

3. Double-click the Set Black Point eyedropper in the Levels dialog box to display the Color Picker. Enter a value of 6 to 8 in the 'Brightness' field (part of the hue, saturation and brightness or HSB controls) and select OK. The precise value is dependent on your printer, paper and ink choice. You can experiment with alternative values later when you have completed the printing project. Move your mouse cursor into the image window and click on the darkest shadow tone that requires visible detail. This action will set your shadow tone.

4. Double-click the Set White Point eyedropper to display the Color Picker again. This time enter a value of 98 in the 'Brightness' field and select OK. Locate the brightest highlight within the image. Do not select a specular highlight such as a light source or a reflection of the light source that should be 255. With the Set White Point eyedropper still selected move into the image window and click on the target highlight to set this as the brightest highlight tone within your image.

Note > When targeting highlights and shadows of a color image a color cast may be introduced into the image if the tones to be targeted are not neutral or desaturated. This can be rectified using the Gray eyedropper to correct any cast introduced.

5. Select the Set Gray Point eyedropper (between the black and white point eyedroppers). Click on a suitable tone you wish to desaturate in an attempt to remove the color cast present in the image (try clicking on the black hair or cooking pots). The neutral tone selected to be the 'Gray Point' can be a dark or light tone within the image. If the tone selected is not representative of a neutral tone the color cast cannot be rectified effectively.

6. Move the Gamma slider to fine-tune the overall brightness of the midtones. Excessive movement of the Gamma slider however will upset the targeted tones set previously.

7. Click OK to apply the tonality changes to the image. When presented with the dialog box that reads 'Save the new target colors as defaults?' you can select 'Yes'. This will ensure that when you use the eyedroppers on your next image all you need do is click once with each of the three eyedroppers.

Project 5

Contrast

One of the most important image adjustment features in a professional photographer's workflow is Curves (a sort of Levels command on steroids). Adobe in their wisdom have now decided to include this feature in their user-friendly Elements version. Color Curves now makes a welcome appearance in the Enhance menu but is not yet available as an adjustment layer. This project shows you several ways to control contrast using adjustment layers to increase your post-production editing power to maximum performance.

RAW IMAGE ON DVD

Create dramatic images by building in some non-destructive contrast

The problem with Brightness/Contrast

If you have been editing your images for some time you will understand that 'Levels' is a superior option to enhance the brightness of your image than the Brightness/Contrast feature. Adjusting the brightness or contrast of an image using the Brightness/Contrast adjustment feature can be very destructive, e.g. if you want to make the shadows brighter and elect to use the Brightness/Contrast control, all of the pixels in the image are made brighter (not just the shadows) - causing the pixels that were already bright to fall off the end of the histogram and lose their detail or become white (level 255).

Moving the Gamma slider to the left in Levels makes the image brighter without clipping the highlights

Using the Levels control you can move the center (Gamma) slider to make the image brighter whilst preserving the black point and white point within the image. This is a far less destructive way to edit the tonality of the image as the highlight detail is preserved and does not become 'clipped'. The only problem with Levels is that it cannot focus its attention on a limited range of tones or increase the midtone contrast of the image.

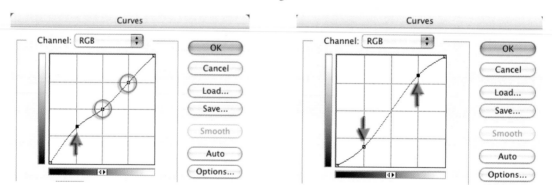

Curves actually start out life as straight diagonal lines. Raising an adjustment point in the middle of the line is like moving the Gamma slider in Levels. Raising the adjustment point makes the midtones brighter whilst lowering the adjustment point makes the tones darker. Additional adjustment points can be used in the shadows (lower left) and highlights (upper right) to control these tones independently of the midtones.

The Curves adjustment feature allows the user to target tones within the image and move them independently, e.g. the user can decide to make only the darker tones lighter whilst preserving the value of both the midtones and the highlights. It is also possible to move the shadows in one direction and the highlights in another. In this way the midtone contrast of the image can be increased without losing valuable detail in either the shadows or the highlights.

Resolving the problem

Now there are four ways to enable you to harness the power of curves in Adobe Elements 5.0. The first way is all new to Elements 5.0. 'Adjust Color Curves' is a user-friendly version of the Curves adjustment feature found in the full version of Photoshop.

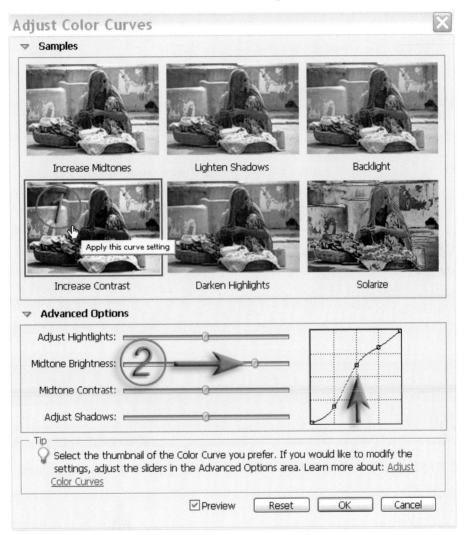

Method 1 - Color Curves

'Adjust Color Curves' can be accessed from the Enhance menu (Enhance > Adjust Color > Adjust Color Curves). The user should first set the levels of the image file by using the techniques outlined in Project 2. Unfortunately 'Adjust Color Curves' is not available as an adjustment layer so it would be advisable to first duplicate the background layer and apply the changes to this duplicate layer. Start by clicking on the thumbnail of your choice and then click on the advanced options to access the sliders that are required to fine-tune the tonality of your image. It may be necessary to add a Hue/Saturation adjustment layer to modify any changes in the color saturation that may have occurred as a result of the Color Curves adjustment.

Accessing curves as an adjustment layer

The second way of using curves, but this time as an adjustment layer, is a bit cheeky and is available if you have access to a multilayered file created in the full version of Photoshop (check out the supporting DVD to download the file used in the example below).

A Photoshop file opened in Elements will allow the user limited functionality to modify the adjustments

Method 2 - Grand theft

One of the great mysteries of life is that although you can't 'create' a Curves adjustment layer in Photoshop Elements you can 'open' an image that already has one. Photoshop Elements allows you to see the effects of the Curves adjustment layer (that was created in the full version of Photoshop), switch it off and on, and lower the opacity of the Curves adjustment layer (enabling you to lower the effect of the adjustment layer gradually). You can also drag this Curves adjustment layer into any other image file that is open in Elements (just click on the adjustment layer thumbnail in the Layers palette and drag it into another image window). Theoretically this means that if you had a single file that was created in Photoshop with a wide range of Curves adjustment layers to suit your everyday image-editing tasks you could use this as a 'Curves resource' - just drag, drop and adjust the opacity to suit the needs of each image you are editing. The sort of adjustment layers that would be particularly useful would be those that enabled the Photoshop Elements user to increase and decrease image contrast, raise or lower shadow brightness independently, and raise or lower highlight brightness independently. If the adjustment layers contain generous adjustments they can be simply tailored to suit each new image-editing task by just lowering or increasing the layer opacity. The adjustment layers are resolution independent, which is another way of saying that they will fit any image, big or small - naughty but very nice!

Method 3 - Gradients

The third version is for users of Elements who want a little more control, have a guilty conscience or prefer to explore the advanced features of the package they have purchased rather than the one they have not. This third method allows you to access the ultimate tonal control that Curves has to offer using a different adjustment feature not really designed for the job but which, when push comes to shove, can be adapted to fit the needs of the cash-strapped image editor seeking quality and control.

1. The first step is to hold down the Alt key whilst selecting the Gradient Map adjustment layer from the Create adjustment layer menu in the Layers palette. This will open the New Layer dialog box. Select 'Luminosity' from the Mode menu and select OK.

2. Click on the third gradient swatch in the presets menu (Black, White). Click on the gradient in the dialog box to open the Gradient Editor.

3. Move the cursor to just below the gray ramp and click to add a 'stop' slightly left of center. Type in 25% as the location and double-click on the color swatch to open the Color Picker.

4. Choose a brightness value of 25% and click OK (ensure a value of 0 is entered in the other two fields of the HSB radio buttons). Add another stop right of center (at a location of approximately 75%) and again click on the color swatch to open the Color Picker. This time choose a brightness value of 75% and again click OK.

5. The 'Black/White' Gradient Map in Luminosity mode will leave the existing tonal values of your image the same as before. The magic starts when you start to drag the stops you created to new positions on the gray ramp. Moving the two sliders further apart will lower the contrast whilst dragging them closer together will increase contrast. A 'Color Midpoint' also appears between the two stops that you are adjusting to allow you to fine-tune your adjustment. In this project drag the two sliders together to increase the contrast but move the color midpoint to the left so that deep shadows do not become too dark. Be amazed - you are exercising absolute control over the brightness values of your image! This technique allows all of the versatility of a Curves adjustment layer when editing the luminosity of your image.

GRADIENT PRESETS ON DVD

PERFORMANCE TIP

When you have created a modified gradient map you can name and add the map to the list of presets for future use. Download the Gradient presets file (Tonal_Gradients.grd) from the supporting DVD and use either your 'Preset Manager' from the Edit menu to add them to your gradient library or load them directly using the Gradient Editor by clicking on the Load button.

Note > Moving stops too close together can create steps or bands in the tonality of your image, creating an effect that is said to be 'posterized' and unnatural. It is important to realize there are limits to how much tonal manipulation an image is capable of handling before the quality suffers.

The Gradient Map adjustment layer set to Luminosity mode acts like a 'Hot-wired' levels adjustment layer. Its advantage is that you can set as many stops or 'sliders' as you like, giving the user total control. Any localized areas that require further attention can simply be masked on the adjacent layer mask and tackled separately on a second Gradient Map layer.

Note > If you have a selection active when you choose the Gradient Map adjustment layer it automatically translates the selection into a layer mask, restricting any adjustments to the selected area.

6. If you are looking to achieve a simple global contrast adjustment the project is complete. If however you want to enhance the image further using more gradients try the following techniques. Choose the 'Gradient tool' from the Tools palette (or type the letter G on the keyboard). Choose the 'Black/White' and 'Linear' options and then drag a gradient from the top of the image window to just below the horizon line. This will shield the sky from the contrast adjustment.

7. We will now balance the tonality in the image by darkening the sky. Click on the Create a New Layer icon in the Layers palette and set the blending mode of this new layer to 'Soft Light'.

8. Ensure that black is the foreground default color (type the letter D on the keyboard) and then choose the 'Foreground to Transparent' gradient. Drag a gradient from the top of the image to a position just below the horizon line. Holding down the Shift key as you drag a gradient, will 'constrain' the gradient to ensure that it is absolutely straight. Try changing the blend mode of this gradient layer to 'Overlay' and 'Multiply' to see the variations of tonality that can be achieved.

9. Yet another way of targeting tones for adjustment is using the Shadows/Highlights adjustment feature. This very useful adjustment feature is not available as an adjustment layer so you will need to create a 'composite' layer of the work carried out so far before you can apply it. This action of creating a composite layer (merging the visible elements from all of the other layers) is called 'Stamp Visible' by professional image editors (Adobe does not list this command in their menus). Select the top layer in the Layers palette and then hold down the Shift+Alt+Ctrl keys whilst you type the letter E on the keyboard. The new layer should appear on top of the layers stack. Double-click the name of the layer to rename it 'Stamp Visible'. Now choose 'Shadows/Highlights' from the Enhance > Adjust Lighting submenu. Set the Lighten Shadows and Darken Highlights sliders to 0 and raise the Midtone Contrast to +30. You can watch the effects of raising this slider by clicking on the Preview box and by viewing the histogram in the Histogram palette.

10. Create another new layer and this time set the blend mode to 'Multiply'. As with the previous gradient you can experiment with alternative blend modes after you have finished creating this second gradient.

Note > You can also set the blend mode for a new layer in the New Layer dialog box.

11. Choose the 'Elliptical Marquee tool' from the Tools palette and choose a large amount of feather (increase the amount of feather as the resolution of the file gets bigger). Draw an elliptical selection in the image window.

Note > You can check how soft this edge is by choosing the 'Selection Brush tool' and clicking on the 'Mask' option.

12. From the Select menu choose 'Inverse' (Shift+Ctrl+I) and then from the Edit menu choose the command 'Fill Selection'. From the Contents section of the dialog box choose 'Foreground Color'. Move the mouse cursor into the image and choose a deep blue color from the image window and then click OK. Lower the opacity of the layer until the vignette is subtle.

PERFORMANCE TIP

Use the Shadows/Highlights adjustment feature on the Stamp Visible layer if the darkening of the shadows becomes excessive as a result of the vignette.

Method 4 - Blend modes

Blend modes are one of the most useful, but least understood, editing features to be found in Elements. One of the groups of layer blend modes that can be applied to layers leads to an increase in contrast of the resulting image, but without the destructive tendencies of the Brightness/Contrast adjustment feature.

1. Open the canyon image from the supporting DVD and hold down the Alt key as you select a Levels adjustment layer. In the New Layer dialog box that opens select 'Soft Light' as the mode. What you now see (if you have the preview box checked in the dialog box) is instant contrast. This contrast is adjustable by moving any of the sliders beneath the histogram. You are able to target shadows, midtones or highlights using these sliders. Select OK to apply the changes.

2. Select 'Black' as the foreground color and with a soft edged brush at a reduced opacity paint out any localized contrast that is not beneficial to the final image. You should see the effects of the painting in the image and in the layer mask of the adjustment layer.

3. Create another new Levels adjustment layer and this time set the blend mode of the layer to 'Multiply'. This blend mode will darken the entire image but we will mask the lower portion of the image later. Focus your attention on just the sky and when you have increased the drama a little select OK. Although we are focussing our attention primarily on the tonality it is still possible to change the color using the individual color channels in the Levels dialog box.

4. Select the 'Gradient tool' from the Tools palette. Select the 'Black, White' option and drag a short gradient from the centre of the image up to the horizon line. The resulting mask will release the lower portion of the image from the grip of the Multiply mode but leave the drama and depth in the sky and distant landscape.

PERFORMANCE TIP

For even more drama and depth duplicate the 'Soft Light' levels adjustment layer (Ctrl+J). Lower the opacity of this layer until you achieve the contrast you are looking for. As with the previous method it is worth keeping the Histogram palette open when making these contrast adjustments so you will notice when the deepest shadows are possibly getting so dark that they will be difficult to print (below level 15). Use the Shadows/Highlights adjustment feature if this becomes the case - either on the background layer or on a new Stamp Visible layer.

Summary

The Gradient Map adjustment layer in Luminosity mode, a Levels adjustment in Soft Light mode and the targeted adjustments offered by the Shadows/Highlights adjustment feature make the need for a Curves adjustment feature redundant. Absolute tonal and color control is just a blend mode away.

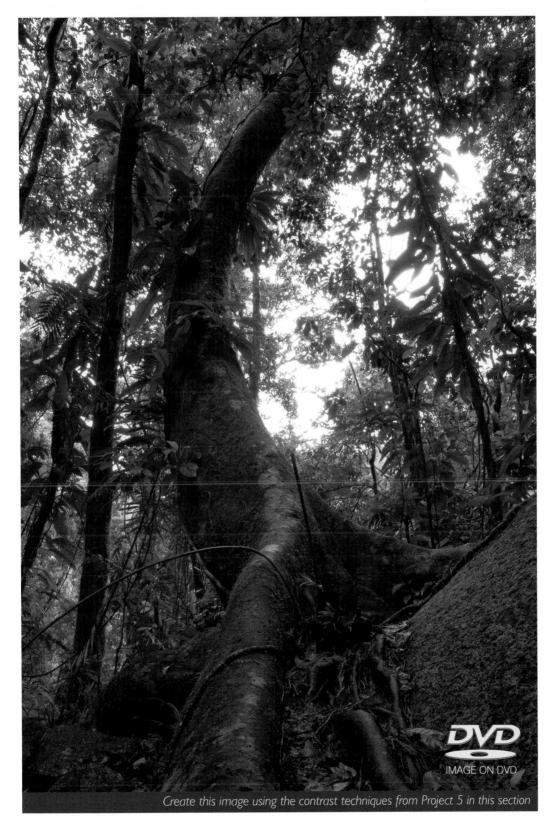

DVD
IMAGE ON DVD

Create this image using the contrast techniques from Project 5 in this section

Project 6

Hue and Saturation

Levels is a powerful adjustment feature for controlling tonality and overall color balance. It cannot however target and control a limited ranges of color values or the saturation of color in general. For this final level of control we need to master the powerful Hue/Saturation adjustment feature. In this project we will target specific colors and then change the hue and saturation of these targeted colors to both repair and creatively enhance images. This technique is not recommended as an alternative to an effective sunscreen or a good broad-rimmed hat!

DVD
RAW IMAGE ON DVD

Hue/Saturation - targeted color adjustment techniques for absolute control

1. From the Layers palette click on the Create Adjustment Layer icon and choose 'Hue/Saturation' to open the Hue/Saturation dialog box.

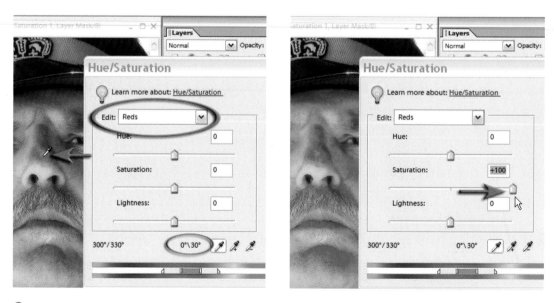

2. From the Edit menu in the Hue/Saturation dialog box choose 'Reds' and then increase the Saturation slider to full strength (+100). Increasing the saturation will help us target a very precise range of reds that we wish to adjust.

3. At the moment all of the warm colors in the face fall in the broad range of reds and are, as a result, excessively saturated. We will now limit or restrict this range of reds so that only those that represent the sunburnt areas of the face are targeted. On the color ramp in the dialog box you will find four sliders. Move the inner two closer together by dragging them towards each other. Then click between the two sliders and move the range of reds to the left slightly (towards the magenta colors). The aim is to make the skin colors in the image window lose their excessive saturation. When this happens they are no longer targeted. Move the outer sliders inwards. As the target colors move closer to these outer sliders they progressively fall beyond any resulting adjustment. When you have effectively targeted the colors of the sunburnt skin, drop the Saturation slider back to '0' and then move the Hue slider to the right to render these colors the same as the rest of the face. Select OK to apply these changes.

4. Select the 'Paintbrush tool' in the Tools palette with black as the foreground color. Choose a soft edged brush from the Options bar and paint in the layer mask in the area of the lips and eyes to return these to their normal and healthy (not sunburnt) color.

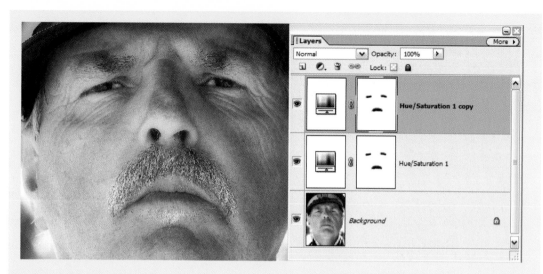

PERFORMANCE TIP

It may be necessary to create a second Hue/Saturation layer to target and fine-tune any remaining colors. Duplicating the adjustment layer by dragging it to the New Layer icon will ensure your masking work is retained. Double-click the Adjustment Layer icon to fine-tune the colors.

Although not as controlled as using a Hue/Saturation adjustment layer, it is possible to make color corrections using the Color Replacement Brush. Sample a 'preferred' color by holding down the Alt key and clicking the mouse. Using a soft edged paintbrush paint over a color that needs to be replaced. It is advised that you work on a duplicate background layer and then lower the opacity of this layer to blend in your corrective surgery.

The Hue/Saturation technique has many applications - from changing one odd bloom in a bouquet of flowers to color coordinating a background color with your subject. If you can't capture your subject against the perfect color backdrop it is usually an option to capture it against a color that has nothing in common with the general skin tones and hair color of your subject, e.g. blue sky or green foliage - just remember to mask the blue or green eyes.

Project 7

Unsharpened

Sharpening

All digital images require sharpening - even if shot on a state-of-the-art digital SLR in focus. Most cameras can sharpen in-camera but the highest quality sharpening is achieved in post-production. Elements will allow you to select the amount and the areas that require sharpening most. For images destined for print the monitor preview is just that - a preview. The actual amount of sharpening required for optimum image quality is usually a little more than looks comfortable on screen - especially when using a TFT monitor (flat panel).

DVD
RAW IMAGE ON DVD

Advanced sharpening - targeted sharpening for maximum impact

The basic concept of sharpening is to send the Unsharp Mask filter on a 'seek and manipulate' mission. The filter is programmed to make the pixels on the lighter side of any edge it finds lighter still, and the pixels on the darker side of the edge darker. Think of it as a localized contrast control. Too much and people in your images start to look radioactive (they glow), not enough and the viewers of your images start reaching for the reading glasses they don't own.

The art of advanced sharpening

The best sharpening techniques are those that prioritize the important areas for sharpening and leave the smoother areas of the image well alone, e.g. sharpening the eyes of a portrait but avoiding the skin texture. These advanced techniques are essential when sharpening images that have been scanned from film or have excessive noise, neither of which needs accentuating by the Unsharp Mask. So let the project begin.

1. Duplicate the background layer. Go to 'Filter > Other > High Pass'. Increase the pixel Radius to around 20 pixels for a 5 or 6 megapixel image. Select OK.

Note > The High Pass filter is sometimes used as an alternative to the Unsharp Mask when the layer is set to 'Overlay' or 'Soft Light' mode. A Radius of 1 to 4 pixels is used in this sharpening technique. In this project we are using the High Pass filter to locate the edges within the image only.

PERFORMANCE TIP

If you have any sharpening options in your capture device it is important to switch them off or set them to minimum or low. The sharpening features found in most capture devices are often very crude when compared to the following technique. It is also not advisable to sharpen images that have been saved as JPEG files using high-compression/low-quality settings. The sharpening process that follows should also come at the end of the editing process, i.e. adjust the color and tonality of the image before starting this advanced sharpening technique.

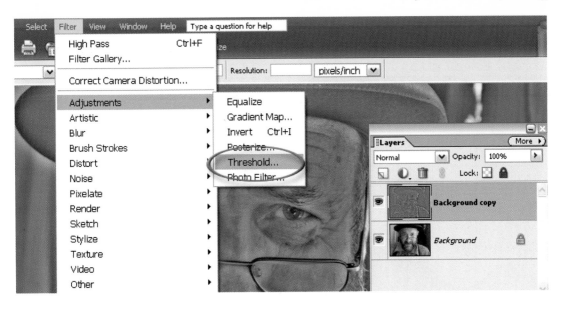

2. Apply a Threshold filter to the High Pass layer from the Filter > Adjustments submenu. The threshold will reduce this layer to two levels - black and white - depending on the brightness value.

3. Drag the slider just below the histogram to isolate the edges that require sharpening. The aim of moving these sliders is to render all of those areas you do not want to sharpen white (or nearly white). Select OK when you are done. You are half-way to creating a sharpening mask. The mask will restrict the sharpening process to the edges only (the edges that you have just defined). Increasing or decreasing the radius in the High Pass filter will render the lines thicker or thinner.

4. Paint out any areas that were not rendered white by the Threshold adjustment that you do not want to be sharpened, e.g. in the portrait used in this example any pixels remaining in the skin away from the eyes, mouth, nose and background were painted over using the Brush tool with 'White' selected as the foreground color.

5. Go to 'Filter > Blur > Gaussian Blur' and apply a 4-pixel Radius to blur this layer. This step will ensure that the sharpening process will fade in slowly rather than have an abrupt edge.

6. Select the 'Magic Eraser tool' in the Tools palette (behind the Eraser tool). Deselect the 'Contiguous' option in the Options bar and then click on any white area within the image. You should be left with only the edge detail on this layer and none of the white areas. The image will appear a little strange until we complete the next couple of steps.

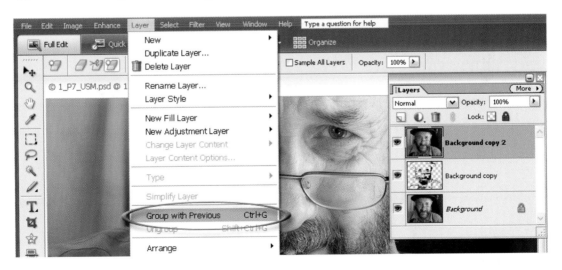

7. Duplicate the background layer and drag this duplicate layer to the top of the layers stack. Ensure the image is zoomed in to 100% for a small image or 50% for a larger print resolution image. From the Layer menu select 'Group with Previous'. The transparent areas on the Threshold layer will act as a mask so only the important areas of the image will appear sharpened.

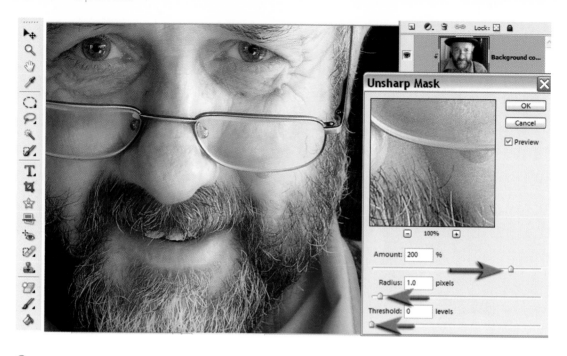

8. Go to 'Filter > Sharpen > Unsharp Mask'. Adjust the Amount slider to between 80 and 150%. This controls how much darker or lighter the pixels at the edges are rendered. Choose an amount slightly more than what looks comfortable on screen if the image is destined for print rather than screen. The Radius slider should be set to 0.5 for screen images and between 1 and 2 pixels for print resolution images. The Radius slider controls the width of the edge that is affected by the Amount slider. The Threshold slider helps the Unsharp Mask decide where the edges are. If the Threshold slider is raised the Unsharp Mask progressively ignores edges of lower contrast.

PERFORMANCE TIP

Before and after sharpening. If you are sharpening an excessively 'noisy' or 'grainy' image the Threshold slider is moved progressively higher to avoid sharpening non-image data. The exact threshold setting is not so critical for this advanced technique.

DVD
IMAGE ON DVD

Create this image using the sharpening techniques from Project 7 in this section

Project 8

| 0 | 3 | 5 | 8 | 10 | 13 | 15 | 18 | 20 | 23 | 26 | 229 | 232 | 235 | 237 | 240 | 242 | 245 | 247 | 250 | 252 | 255 |

Printing

Creating high-quality prints using desktop inkjet printers can be a mystifying and costly experience. Matching the colors of the print to those that appear on your monitor can be an infuriating experience. This example of a printing workflow may help you overcome some of the obstacles you may be encountering and enable you to attain perfect prints.

PRINT RESOLUTION IMAGE ON DVD

Adopt a color management workflow that delivers predictable prints every time

Most professionals use the Adobe RGB workspace when images are destined for print rather than web viewing. Set your own workspace by going to Edit > Color Settings prior to editing your own folio images. Use the Adobe Gamma utility, which can be found in the 'Control Panels' of your operating system, to guide you through the calibration process for your monitor or, better still, invest in a monitor calibration device that ensures maximum performance. Now follow these six simple steps to turn your edited images into folio masterpieces.

EPSON StatusMonitor

Remaining Ink level

EPSON recommended ink cartridge
Black : T026   Color : T027

Click the image of the ink cartridge to display
information about the current cartridge.

1. Preflight checklist

In an attempt to make the first time not too memorable, for all the wrong reasons, check that your ink cartridges are not about to run out of ink and that you have a plentiful supply of good quality paper (same surface and same make). It is also worth starting to print when there are several hours of daylight left, as window light (without direct sun) is the best light to judge the color accuracy of the prints. If you are restricted to printing in the evening it may be worthwhile checking out 'daylight' globes that offer a more 'neutral' light source than tungsten globes or fluorescent tubes. It is also important to position the computer's monitor so that it is not reflecting any light source in the room (including the direct illumination from windows and skylights). If your monitor is reflecting a brightly colored wall or window then consider shifting your furniture.

Note > Refilling your ink cartridges and using cheap paper are not recommended for absolute quality and consistency.

2. Keeping a record

RECORD SHEET ON DVD

Project	Portrait	Sept 22/04
Image File	TIFF	220 ppi
Paper	Epson	Matte HW
Inks	Epson	AUG 04
Colour Management	Adobe ☐	Printer ☑
Profiles	N/A	Same As Source
Printer Settings	Matte HW	Best Photo
Colour Controls	Photo-realistic	+4 Saturation

The settings of the translation process (all the buttons and options that will be outlined next), the choice of paper, the choice of ink and the lighting conditions used to view the print will all have enormous implications for the color that you see on the printed page. The objective when you have achieved a color match is to maintain consistency over the process and materials so that it can be repeated with each successive print. It is therefore important to keep a track of the settings and materials used.

There is only one thing more infuriating than not being able to achieve accuracy and that is achieving it once and not being sure of how you did it. Some words of advice ... WRITE IT DOWN!

Note > A template for the print record sheet is available on the supporting DVD.

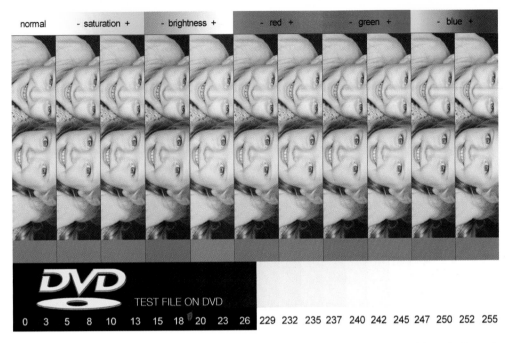

normal	- saturation +	- brightness +	- red +	- green +	- blue +

TEST FILE ON DVD

0   3   5   8   10   13   15   18   20   23   26   229 232 235 237 240 242 245 247 250 252 255

Use the test file to help you target the perfect color balance quickly and efficiently

3. Preparing a test print

Start the printing process by selecting 'Print with Preview' from the File menu. As discussed previously there are several methods of printing. There is no one road. In order to discover a workflow that suits your own setup it is recommended that you use a test file that has a broad range of colors of varying saturations. Use a test file that incorporates a range of saturated colors, neutral grays and skin tones. If this file prints perfectly you can be confident that subsequent prints using the same media and settings will follow true to form. The test print file in the illustration above is available on the supporting DVD. It will help you target your optimum shadow and highlight points, and stop you from chasing what initially appears to be a color cast and in the end turns out to be a blocked ink jet.

Note > There is an old saying, 'quality in - quality out'. You must check that each image you print has been optimized for printing. The file's histogram should be optimized and any obvious color cast removed.

4. Print

Select 'Print' from the File menu. Although Adobe has the industry standard color management engine it is only effective if you have a custom-made profile for your printer/paper combination. The latest photo printers are however more than up to the task of handling the color management.

1. Click 'Page Setup' at the bottom of the dialog box to select paper size and orientation
2. Deselect the 'Center Image' checkbox
3. Drag the image preview to one side of the page to save printing paper
4. Click on the Show More Options box to expand the dialog box
5. Select the 'Printer Color Management' option in the Color Management section
6. Select 'Print'.

Note > If you have calibrated your printer and have a unique profile for your printer/ paper combination then you should select this as the printer profile and turn off the color management in the printer.

5. Printer driver

Printer drivers are specific to your make and model of printer. The options outlined below will act as a guide for the settings in your own printer driver. Look for the same or similar options in your Printer Driver dialog box:

1. You may need to select 'Properties' in the first dialog box to access the printer settings
2. Select the 'Advanced' option if there is one to access ALL of the settings
3. Select the paper you are using from the Media Type or Paper Options menu
4. Select the maximum dpi from the Print Quality menu or any option that indicates that the 'Best Photo' quality option has been selected
5. Select 'Color Controls' from the Color Management menu (you should see the Magenta, Cyan and Yellow color sliders)
6. Select 'Print'.

The options for 'Printer Color Management' in an Epson printer driver for a PC

The printer is now handling the color management. Once the test file has been printed you can make an assessment of what changes need to be made before printing a modified or 'tweaked' version. Be sure to let the test print dry for at least 10 to 15 minutes before making an assessment of the color and tonal values as these may change quite dramatically. Subtle changes can continue to occur for several hours during the drying process. See 'Analyzing the test print' when assessing whether any changes need to be made to the first test print. To speed up and simplify the procedure for subsequent prints a 'custom setting' or 'preset' can be resaved in the printer driver once you have achieved accuracy by fine-tuning the color sliders. Name the custom setting incorporating the paper surface, e.g. Matte HW-PCM (printer color management).

Note > The precise wording of the options in the printer drivers may vary between different manufacturers and models of printer.

6. Analyzing the test print

View the print using soft window light (not direct sunlight) when the print is dry, and try to ascertain any differences between the print and the screen image in terms of hue (color), saturation and brightness. Any differences may be attributed to inaccuracies in your initial monitor calibration.

1. Check that the color swatches at the top of the image are saturated and printing without tracking marks or banding (there should be a gradual transition of color). If there is a problem with missing colors, tracking lines or saturation, clean the printer heads using the printer guidelines.

2. View the skin tones to assess the appropriate level of saturation. The lower and higher saturation swatches have a –10 and +10 adjustment applied using Photoshop's Hue/Saturation adjustment.

3. View the gray tones directly beneath the images of the children to determine if there is a color cast present in the image. The five tones on the extreme left are desaturated in the image file. If these print as gray then no color correction is required. If however one of the gray tones to the right (which have color adjustments applied) appears to be gray then a color cast is present.

4. Find the tone that appears to be desaturated (the color cast corresponds with the color swatches at the top of the test file). Apply this color correction to the next print. For example, if the plus green strip appears to print with no color cast (the gray swatches on the far left will therefore be printing with a magenta cast) then a 1.1 Gamma adjustment in the green channel is required for the next test print. Alternatively, a minus value can be entered in the Magenta slider in the 'Color Controls' in the printer dialog box.

Note > Each of the color strips in the test image has the same Gamma adjustment applied using the RGB channels. The correction necessary can be made using the Levels dialog box by sliding the Gamma slider to 0.9 or 1.1 in the corresponding color channel.

7. Maximizing shadow and highlight detail

Examine the base of the test strip to establish the optimum highlight and shadow levels that can be printed with the media you have chosen to use. If the shadow tones between level 10 and level 20 are printing as black then you should establish a Levels adjustment layer to resolve the problem in your Adobe software. The bottom left-hand slider should be moved to the right to reduce the level of black ink being printed. This should allow dark shadow detail to be visible in the second print. A less common problem is highlight values around 245 not registering on the media. However if this is a problem, the highlight slider can be moved to the left to encourage the printer to apply more ink.

Note > It is important to apply these Output level adjustments to an adjustment layer only as these specific adjustments apply only to the output device you are currently testing.

PERFORMANCE TIP

Materials
Start by using the printer manufacturer's recommended ink and paper.
Use premium grade 'photo paper' for maximum quality.

Monitor
Position your monitor so that it is clear of reflections.
Let your monitor warm up for a while (up to 30 minutes) before judging image quality.
Select a target white point or color temperature of 6500 K (D65).
Calibrate your monitor using a calibration device if available.

Adobe
Set the Color Settings of the Adobe software.
Select 'Let printer determine colors'.
Use a 6-ink inkjet printer or better for maximum quality.
Select the 'Media Type' in the Printer Software dialog box.
Select a high dpi setting (1440dpi or greater) or 'Best Photo' quality setting.

Proofing
Allow print to dry and use daylight to assess color accuracy of print.

part 2

enhance

Project 1

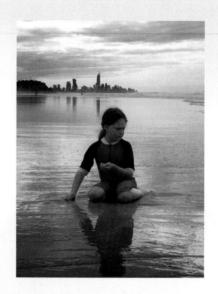

Depth of Field

The Gaussian Blur filter can be used creatively to blur distracting backgrounds. Most digital cameras achieve greater depth of field (more in focus) at the same aperture when compared to their 35 mm film cousins, due to their comparatively small sensor size. This is great in some instances but introduces unwelcome detail and distractions when the attention needs to be firmly fixed on the subject.

There is often a lot to think about during the capture of an image and the time required to consider the appropriate aperture and shutter speed combination for the desired visual outcome often gets the elbow. Elements can, however, come to the rescue and drop a distracting background into a murky sea of out-of-focus oblivion. Problems arise when the resulting image, all too often, looks manipulated rather than realistic. A straight application of the Gaussian Blur filter will have a tendency to 'bleed' strong tonal differences and saturated colors into the background fog, making the background in the image look more like a watercolor painting than a photograph. The Gaussian Blur filter will usually require some additional work if the post-production technique is not to become too obvious.

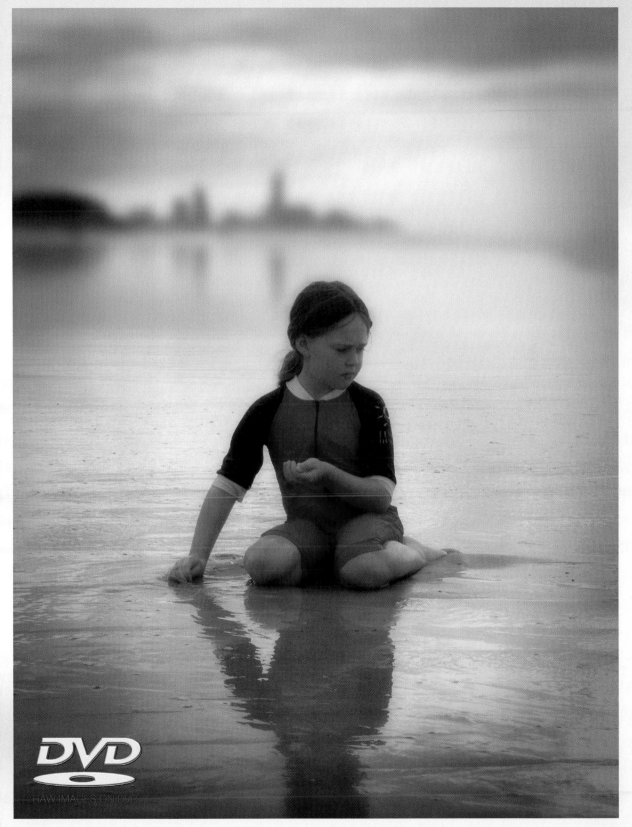

DVD

Decrease the depth of field to emphasize your subject

1. Not all subjects lend themselves to automated extraction processes. Professionals using the full version of Photoshop often make use of 'Channels' to start the process of creating a mask where there is not sufficient contrast between the subject and its background. As channels are off limits for Photoshop Elements users (Photoshop Elements uses them but you are not allowed to see them) we need to use a workaround. We can borrow or hijack a layer mask from an adjustment layer for our purposes in this project.

Create a Levels adjustment layer. Click OK without making any adjustments (we need the mask rather than the adjustment that this layer offers). From the Select menu choose 'All' (Ctrl+A). Choose 'Copy Merged' from the Edit menu (this copies everything that is visible rather than everything that is on the current layer - very useful, as there are no pixels on the adjustment layer!) Now if we select 'Paste' from the Edit menu the pixels are not pasted into the layer mask (even though it has been selected) they are pasted into a new layer. To paste them into the layer mask we need to hold down the Alt key and then click on the layer mask. This is the keyboard shortcut for viewing the contents of the layer mask. Only in this state will Photoshop allow us to paste the pixels from the clipboard into the layer mask.

2. It is possible to modify, manipulate and massage the contents of the layer mask into something that will prove effective for separating the background from the subject (the essential ingredient if we are going to tamper with the depth of field in this image). To increase the contrast of this mask we will apply a Levels adjustment to this mask to start the ball rolling (go to the Enhance > Adjust Lighting submenu or use the keyboard shortcut Ctrl+L). Your objective is to render the background white (out of focus) and the subject black (in focus). The Highlight slider can be dragged to the left to clip all highlight tones to white. The Shadow slider can be dragged to the right to render all shadow tones black. Drag the Gamma slider whichever way gives the best outline to the main subject.

3. Painting in Photoshop is not everybody's flavor of the month. There is however a Magic Paintbrush technique when masking that makes it a far less painful procedure. Switch the blend mode of the Paintbrush tool to 'Overlay' in the Options bar and set the foreground and background colors to their default setting in the Tools palette. It's that simple! When you now paint in the layer mask all the gray tones are progressively rendered lighter or darker tones depending whether you are painting with white or black. The magic lies in the fact that black has no effect on the lightest tones and white has no effect on the darkest tones in Overlay mode. Try it! Paint with black in the white areas: result - no effect. Switching between black and white (press x on the keyboard) and repeating the work in some areas results in a vastly improved mask with very little effort. Now switch back to Normal mode (the magic has its limits) and with steady hands touch up all of the areas in the distance that refuse to respond to the magic. You can leave all of the areas in the immediate foreground and around the base of the girl black.

4. Focus is not a brick wall, i.e. it does not start and end suddenly - it gradually fades in and out. Think Gradient tool when you are thinking of fading between masked and unmasked. Choose the 'Gradient tool' in the Tools palette with white as the foreground color. Choose the 'Foreground to Background' and 'Linear' options in the Options bar. Drag a gradient from the base of the image to the point where the girl is in contact with the sand.

5. To further ensure we don't end up with an unnatural shift in focus it is important to soften the edge of the subject a little. Apply a 1 or 2 pixel Gaussian Blur (Filter > Blur > Gaussian Blur) before proceeding with the gradients in this mask.

 Note > The TIFF file for this project has a saved selection (Selection > Load Selection > DOF). Creating a layer mask with this active selection will automatically create the layer mask in step 5.

6. Duplicate the adjustment layer that you are working on by dragging it to the New Layer icon in the Layers palette (multiple masks will give us a few options later on). Alt+Click the layer mask of the 'Duplicate' levels adjustment layer to view the contents of the new mask. With the Gradient tool still selected choose black as the foreground color and the 'Foreground/Transparent' and 'Reflected Gradient' options in the Options bar. Drag a gradient from the base of the girl to somewhere around the horizon line in the distance (holding down the Shift key as you drag will constrain the gradient so that it is not crooked). The gradient will extend both sides of the girl. This will become our plane of focus. Alt+Click on the layer mask to exit the layer mask view.

7. Drag the background layer to the New Layer icon and then drag it to the top of the layers stack (shortcuts - Ctrl+J to duplicate background layer, then Ctrl+Shift+] to move this duplicate layer to the top of the layers stack). Now apply the Gaussian Blur filter to this layer. How much you drop the focus is pretty much a subjective step. Very shallow depth of field is achieved with larger apertures, a close vantage point and larger format cameras. If you are generous with the pixel radius in the Gaussian Blur filter the image will appear as though it was created with a large format film camera - something that is impossible to achieve with a digital compact unless you are shooting an insect or flower in macro mode. At this stage the entire image will be subjected to the effects of the blur.

8. Group this blurred layer with the adjustment layer below (Layer > Group or Ctrl+G). If the level of blur required was difficult to assess in the last step it is possible to group this layer prior to applying the Gaussian Blur filter. The power of this effect is to remove distracting background clutter from the image, isolate the subject and keep the focus entirely on the focal point of the image. Unfortunately the effect at this stage has a few shortcomings. The effect of blurring the background has bled some of the darker and more saturated tones into the lighter more desaturated background. A tell-tale halo is forming that indicates this effect has been achieved in post-production rather than in-camera.

9. Wherever there is a problem there is usually a 'fixit' waiting to be found. Photoshop CS2 users have a beautiful Lens Blur filter that renders this effect without the halo. Elements users can fix the problem in a couple of additional steps. The first involves Ctrl+Clicking the first adjustment layer mask (the one without the reflected gradient) to load the mask as a selection. Then select the background layer and copy these pixels to the clipboard. Select the top layer and then select 'Paste' from the Edit menu (Ctrl+V). This will reduce but not eliminate the bleeding problem.

10. The problem is finally resolved by careful application of the Clone Stamp tool. Select the Blur layer, the Clone Stamp tool, the 'Lighten' and 'Aligned' options in the Options bar. Reduce the opacity of the tool and hold down the Alt key as you select some pixels further away from the edge, where the bleed has not extended to, and paint these pixels back into the affected border regions. Switch from Lighten to Darken modes if you encounter brighter tones bleeding into a darker background.

11. Final adjustment to the tone and sharpness is made by stamping the visible elements to a new layer on top of the layers stack ('Select > Select All' then 'Edit > Copy Merged' then 'Edit > Paste' or Ctrl+Alt+Shift and then type the letter E).

PERFORMANCE TIP

Adjustment layer masks can also be hijacked and used to mask either sharpening effects or the effects of a Shadows/Highlights adjustment (not available as a layer adjustment). If you need to see the mask at the same time as the image hold down the Shift key at the same time as holding down the Alt key when you click on the layer mask thumbnail. This allows you to paint the mask accurately to your subject. Hold down the Shift and Alt keys as you click on the layer mask thumbnail to return the view to normal. In this example the Unsharp Mask is removed from the girl but is left to sharpen the ripples of water surrounding her.

 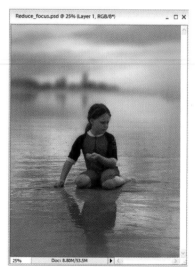

12. The viewer's attention can be further restricted to the central subject by adding a subtle vignette so that the image progressively gets brighter towards the center (we are visually drawn to the light). Create a new layer and then use the Elliptical Marquee tool and feather the resulting selection by 100 pixels.

Note > View the selection as a mask (Selection Brush tool with the 'Mask' option selected) as you choose a feather radius to gain a visual idea of an appropriate amount of feather.

13. Invert the selection (Select > Inverse), select a dark color from the image using the Eyedropper tool and then choose 'Edit > Fill Selection > Foreground Color' (Alt+Backspace). Set the blend mode of the layer to 'Overlay' or 'Multiply' and reduce the opacity so the vignette sits on the edge of your perception for the most subtle effect.

FUTURE DEVELOPMENTS
SHIFTING FOCUS

If digital cameras are eventually able to record distance information at the time of capture this could be used in the creation of an automatic depth map (the CS2 Lens Blur filter can already use channels or layer masks to create automated depth of field effects but the channel must still be created manually using the techniques outlined in this project). Choosing the most appropriate depth of field could be relegated to post-production image editing in a similar way to how the white balance is set in camera RAW.

IMAGE ON DVD

Project 2

GRADIENT PRESET ON DVD

Shafts of Light

Here we explore the science of making good photographs even more memorable. Discover how to add drama to your landscape images using the 'Fingers of God' tool (aka the Gradient tool with customized settings). Creating effective landscape images is not exactly rocket science. Choose a beautiful landscape just after dawn, or just before sunset, and add dramatic natural lighting to create emotive and memorable landscape images.

Let there be light - create dramatic lighting effects to enhance the drama of your images

Clear blue skies are great for holidays on the beach but the best natural lighting for photography is provided by broken or filtered sunlight through partial cloud cover. The most memorable of all lighting is when shafts of light break through the clouds. Finding partial cloud cover when the sun is low is relatively easy, being present when shafts of light flood your selected vista however can be an elusive and rare event. This final and quintessential ingredient requires patience, persistence and good fortune - or a good helping of post-production editing courtesy of Photoshop Elements.

1. Choose the 'Magic Wand' in the Tools palette and make a selection that excludes the sky (the region not selected will play host to the shafts of light). Increase the 'Tolerance' in the Options bar and deselect the 'Contiguous' option prior to clicking the foreground with the Magic Wand to increase the size of your selection. Hold down the Shift key and click additional areas or select the Grow command from the Select menu to expand the selection.

Note > Deselecting the 'Contiguous' option will allow the Magic Wand to select all similar pixels, even if they are not adjoining the area clicked on.

2. Choose the 'Selection Brush tool' from the Tools palette and choose the 'Mask' option from the Options bar. The 'Mask' option enables you to see your selection as a painted mask so you can easily see what areas are selected. Choose an appropriate brush size and paint to add areas of the sky missed by the Magic Wand. Hold down the Alt key as you paint to remove any areas of the mask (and resulting selection) that are not required.

Note > You can choose an alternative color for the overlay mask and adjust the opacity in the Options bar to make the selection process easier.

3. Go to the Select menu and choose 'Save Selection'. You can give your selection a name to help you locate this for a later stage in the editing process. Choose 'Deselect' from the Select menu.

4. From the top of the Layers palette click on the Create New Fill or Adjustment Layer icon and choose 'Levels' from the menu. Drag the central Gamma slider in the Levels dialog box to the left to substantially brighten the image. The tonality for the majority of the image will be returned to normal by creating a sophisticated layer mask for this adjustment layer in the next stages of the tutorial.

5. Set the foreground color to black. Select the 'Gradient' tool and the 'Foreground to Transparent' gradient. Click on the Edit button in the Options bar.

6. Clicking on the Edit button opens the Gradient Editor dialog box. Click on the 'Transparent Stripes' gradient. Edit the gradient using the following pointers. The aim of editing the gradient is to make the stripes irregular widths with softer edges to emulate the irregular and softer nature of shafts of light. The white stops on the top of the editing ramp indicate full transparency whilst the black stops indicate full opacity of the foreground color. Click and drag the stops into groups of four. A white stop should be on either end of a grouping of four with two black stops next to each other in the middle. Moving the black stops further apart will broaden the stripe. Moving the white stop further away from the central black stops will broaden the area of transition between full opacity and full transparency. To add a stop hold down the Alt key and drag an existing stop a short distance. To remove a stop drag a stop away from the gradient ramp. To add this modified gradient to the presets click on the New button and give your shafts of light a suitable name (don't worry that the shafts are colored black for the moment). This gradient can be loaded from the Preset that is available on the DVD.

Note > A black stop can be changed to a white stop or vice-versa by clicking on the stop and then adjusting the Opacity slider in the bottom Stops section of the Gradient Editor.

7. Make sure the 'Linear' gradient option is selected in the Options bar and set the opacity to 100% and the mode to 'Normal'. The foreground color should still be set to black. Click on the left side of the image window and drag your mouse cursor to the right side of the image window. The length of the line you draw will be the initial width of the shafts although this can be modified using the Transform command outlined in the following step.

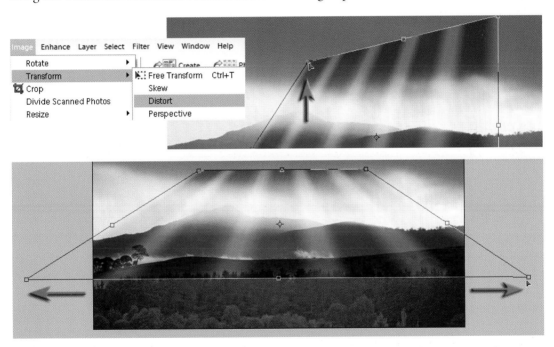

8. From the Image menu select 'Distort' from the Transform submenu. Click on each of the corner handles and drag them to fan the shafts of light. Move the cursor into the Transform bounding box, and click and drag the bounding box to reposition the shafts of light. When you're satisfied with the shape, double-click inside the distorted bounding box to accept the transformation.

Note > You may need to extend the image window so that you can drag the corner handles to the required angle.

9. Go to the Filter menu and select 'Invert' from the Adjustments submenu. This will turn the black stripes to white and return the brightness level of the rest of the image to normal. The next step will aim to limit the shafts of light to the selection made at the start of the tutorial.

10. From the Select menu choose 'Load Selection' and load the selection saved at the start of the tutorial. From the Edit menu choose the 'Fill Selection' command and select 'Black' as the fill color and then select OK. This will further limit the shafts of light to the desired location.

11. Select the Gradient tool and choose the 'Foreground to Transparent' gradient. Drag a short gradient from the start of the shafts of light to conceal their hard edges.

12. Soften the mask further by going to the Filter menu and choosing 'Gaussian Blur' from the Blur submenu. Choose a pixel Radius that will soften the edges of the mask so the cut-off of the lighting behind the distant hill is subtle. The only problem with this technique is that it is almost too effective and therefore tempting to sneak it into too many images in your personal folio. When this happens the cat will be well and truly out of the bag.

Note > It is possible to increase the intensity of the shafts of light by switching the blend mode of the adjustment layer to 'Screen'. Adjust the opacity to fine-tune the effect.

PERFORMANCE TIP

Create a focal point by introducing some birds that will be silhouetted against the shafts of light. Open the second image file and drag the thumbnail from the background layer (in the Layers palette) into the image window of the project. Holding down the Shift key when you let go of the file will center it in the host image. Switching the blend mode to 'Multiply' will render the white background of this layer invisible. Good just got better.

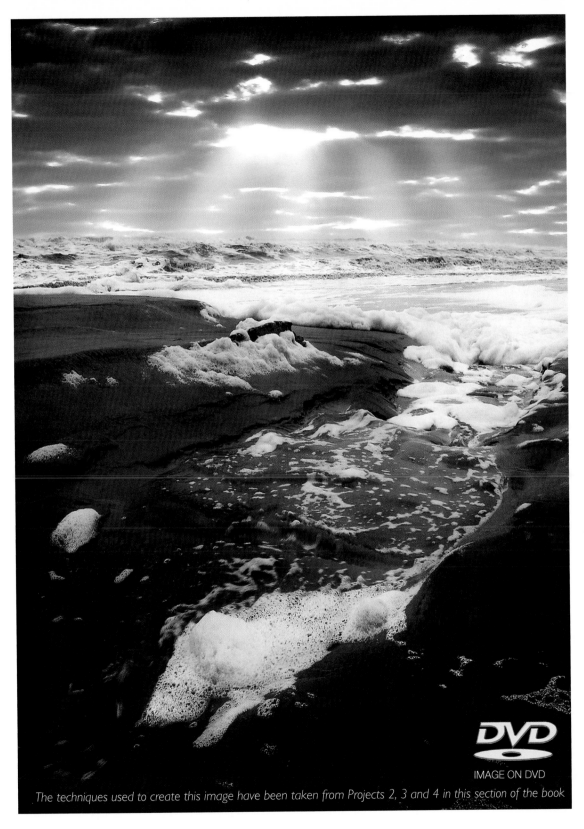

IMAGE ON DVD

The techniques used to create this image have been taken from Projects 2, 3 and 4 in this section of the book

Project 3

The original color image and the result of choosing the less than satisfactory Remove Color command

DVD

16 BIT/CHANNEL IMAGE
ON SUPPORTING DVD

Black and white - when 'luminance' is more important than color. Original image by Michael Wennrich

Black and White

When color film arrived over half a century ago the pundits who presumed that black and white images would die a quick death were surprisingly mistaken. Color is all very nice but sometimes the rich tonal qualities that we can see in the work of the photographic artists are something certainly to be savoured. Can you imagine an Ansel Adams masterpiece in color? If you can - read no further.

The conversion from color to black and white

The creation of dramatic black and white photographs from your color images is a little more complicated than simply converting your image to Grayscale mode or choosing the Desaturate command. Ask any professional photographer who is skilled in the art of black and white and you will discover that crafting tonally rich images requires a little knowledge about how different color filters effect the resulting tonality of a black and white image.

'Convert to Black and White' allows you to mix the tonal differences present in the color channels. It's a little like Color Variations to use (see page 14). Simply pick a style, the intensity and click on the thumbnails to create your own custom conversion

As strange as it may seem, screwing on a color filter for capturing images on black and white film has traditionally been an essential ingredient to the recipe for success. The most popular color filter in the black and white photographer's kit bag, which is used for the most dramatic effect, is the red filter. The effect of the red filter is to lighten all things that are red and darken all things that are not red in the original scene. The result is a print with considerable tonal differences compared to an image shot without a filter. Is this a big deal? Well, yes it is - blue skies are darkened and skin blemishes are lightened. That's a winning combination for most landscape and portrait photographers wanting to create black and white masterpieces.

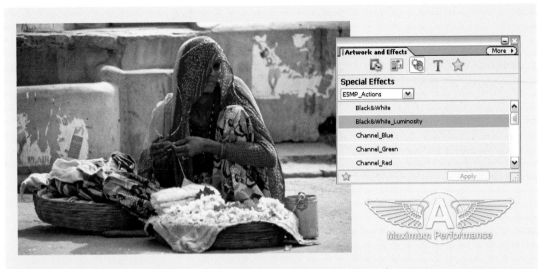

PERFORMANCE TIP

The Maximum Performance Actions included on the DVD includes a series of automated black and white conversions (see the introductory section for installing Maximum Performance Actions). The Black&White_Luminosity action creates a single monochrome layer containing the Luminosity values of the RGB file (usually a superior black and white conversion when compared with the Remove Color command. The Red, Green and Blue channel actions allows you to place one of the three color channels as a black and white layer. These actions would also be useful for accessing the best contrast in order to create a mask as in the Depth of Field project.

In the image to the left the red channel was used as this offered the best detail in the dark skin tones. The contrast was then increased by duplicating the layer and switching the blend mode to 'Soft Light'. The opacity of this duplicate layer was then dropped to 30%. A vignette was added to complete the project

The Convert to Black and White command (Enhance > Convert to Black and White) allows the user to selectively mix the differences in the tonality present in the three color channels but unfortunately it is not available as an adjustment layer. This means we are unable to make use of the layer mask that typically comes with an adjustment layer. It also means that we would be unable to modify the color conversion at a later date without returning to the original color file. This approach to the conversion (although vastly superior to anything present in previous versions of the software) limits the usefulness of the technique for those users who wish to extract the maximum amount of control and flexibility over the process of black and white conversion. The famous digital guru, Russell Preston Brown, has come up with a workaround that enables us to retain complete control over the black and white conversion using multiple adjustment layers.

1. Drag the Layers palette from the Palette Bin (this will be your command center for this technique). Click on the Adjustment Layer icon in the Layers palette and scroll down the list to select and create a Hue/Saturation adjustment layer. You will make no adjustments for the time being but simply select OK to close the dialog box. Set the blend mode of this adjustment layer to 'Color'.

2. Create a second Hue/Saturation adjustment layer. Slide the Saturation slider all the way to the left (minus 100) to desaturate the image. Select OK. The image will now appear as if you had performed a simple Convert to Grayscale or Desaturate (remove color) command.

Note > This second adjustment layer should be sitting on top of the layers stack.

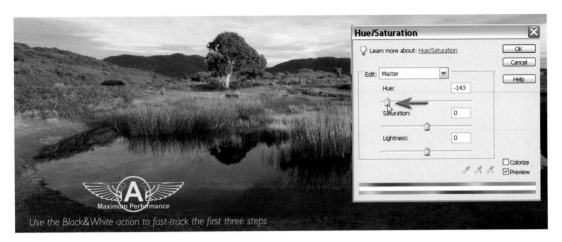

Use the Black&White action to fast-track the first three steps

3. Select the first Hue Saturation layer that you created and double-click the layer thumbnail to reopen the Hue/Saturation dialog box. Move the Hue slider in this dialog box to the left. Observe the changes to the tonality of the image as you move the slider. Blues will be darkest when the slider is moved to a position around −150. Select OK. The drama of the image will probably have been improved quite dramatically already but we can take this further with some dodging and burning.

Note > A Maximum Performance Action is available to fast-track the first three steps in this project (see the introductory section for installing and using Maximum Performance Actions).

4. Click on the New Layer icon in the Layers palette. Set the blend mode of the layer to 'Overlay'. Set the default 'Foreground and Background' colors in the Tools palette and then select the 'Gradient tool'. In the Options bar select the 'Foreground (black) to Transparent' and 'Linear' gradient options.

5. Drag a gradient from the top of the image window to the horizon line. This will have the effect of drawing the viewer into the image and will create an increased sense of drama. Lower the opacity of the layer if the effect is too strong and duplicate the layer if you want to increase the drama further.

6. Press the Alt key and click on the New Layer icon. In the New Layer dialog box set the blend mode to 'Overlay' or 'Soft Light' and select the 'Neutral Color' option. Select the 'Brush tool' and select a soft edged brush from the Options bar and lower the opacity to 10-15%. A layer that is 50% Gray in Overlay or Soft Light mode is invisible. This gray layer will be used to dodge and burn your image non-destructively, i.e. you are not working on the actual pixels of your image. Paint onto the gray layer with black selected as the foreground color to burn (darken) the image in localized areas or switch to white to dodge (lighten) localized areas. You can fill or paint using selections to control the dodging and burning process if required.

7. Select the top layer and then create a Levels adjustment layer (one adjustment layer to rule them all) to sit above all of the other layers. Make sure the histogram extends all the way between the black and white sliders. Move the sliders in to meet the histogram if this is not the case.

PERFORMANCE TIP

Try experimenting with the introduction of some of the original color. Duplicate the background layer by dragging it to the New Layer icon. Then drag the background copy further up the layers stack to a position just below the Levels adjustment layer. Reduce the opacity of this layer and set the blend mode to 'Color' to let the black and white version introduce the drama once more.

Project 4

Maximum Performance

Toning

Burning, toning, split-grade printing and printing through your mother's silk stockings are just some of the wonderful, weird and positively wacky techniques used by the traditional masters of the darkroom waiting to be exposed (or ripped off) in this tantalizing digital project designed to pump up the mood and ambience of the flat and downright dull. The tonality of the project image destined for the toning table will be given a split personality. The shadows will be gently blurred to add depth and character whilst the highlights will be lifted and left with full detail for emphasis and focus. Selected colors will then be mapped to the new tonality to establish the final mood.

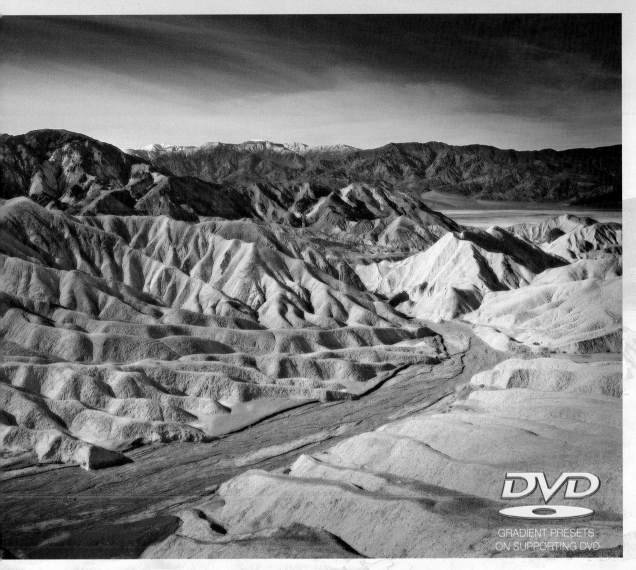

DVD

Death Valley, Arizona. Original image courtesy of Michael Wennrich
Toned images - exploring the land between black and white and color

It probably comes as no small surprise that 'color' injects images with mood and emotional impact. Photographers, however, frequently work on images that are devoid of color because of the tonal control they are able to achieve in traditional processing and printing techniques. Toning the resulting 'black and white' images keeps the emphasis on the play of light and shade but lets the introduced colors influence the final mood. With the increased sophistication and control that digital image-editing software affords us, we can now explore the 'twilight zone' between color and black and white as never before. The original image has the potential to be more dramatic and carry greater emotional impact through the controlled use of tone and color.

1. For the best results choose an image where the directional lighting (low sunlight or window light) has created interesting highlights and shadows that gently model the three-dimensional form within the image. Adjust the levels if necessary so that the tonal range extends between the Shadow and Highlight sliders.

2. Bright areas of tone within the image can be distracting if they are not part of the main subject matter. It is common practice when working in a black and white darkroom to 'burn' the sky darker so that it does not detract the viewer's attention from the main focal point of the image. In the project image the overly bright sky detracts from the drama in the foreground hills. Make an initial selection of the sky using the Magic Wand tool, feather the selection by 2 pixels (Select > Feather) and then save the selection (Select > Save). Create an empty new layer and set the blend mode in the Layers palette to 'Overlay'. Click on the foreground color swatch in the Tools palette to open the Color Picker. Select a deep blue and select OK. In the Options bar select the 'Foreground to Transparent' and 'Linear Gradient' options. Drag a gradient from the top of the image to just below the horizon line to darken the sky. Holding down the Shift key as you drag constrains the gradient keeping it absolutely vertical.

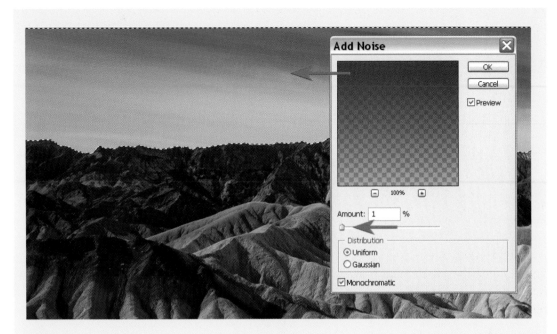

PERFORMANCE TIP

After adding a gradient it is recommended that a small amount of noise is added to the gradient to match the noise quality of the rest of the image and to prevent banding - both on screen and in the final print. Go to 'Filter > Noise > Add Noise'. A small amount of 1 or 2% of monochromatic noise will usually do the trick.

3. Duplicate the background layer (the one without the gradient) and then drag it to the top of the layers stack. Select 'Remove Color' from the Enhance > Adjust Color menu or alternatively you could use a Hue/Saturation adjustment layer and move the Saturation slider all the way to the left.

4. Hold down the Alt key on the keyboard and click on the Create Adjustment Layer icon. In the New Layer dialog box check the 'Group With Previous Layer' option. Click OK to open the Levels dialog box.

5. Drag the Highlight slider to the left until most of the highlights disappear. Move the Gamma slider (the one in the middle) until you achieve good contrast in the midtones of the image. Move the Shadow Output slider to the right to prevent the deeper shadow tones from becoming too dark when the blend mode is applied in the next step. Select OK to apply the Levels adjustment.

6. In the Layers palette switch the mode of this Grayscale layer to 'Multiply' to blend these modified shadow tones back into the color image.

7. Go to the Select menu and choose 'Load Selection'. Choose your saved selection from step 2 and choose the 'Invert' option. Go to 'Filter > Blur > Gaussian Blur' and increase the Radius to spread and soften the shadow tones (approximately 6 pixels). With the preview on you will be able to see the effect as you raise the amount of blur. Go to 'View > Zoom' In to take a closer look at the effect you are creating. The selection will prevent the dark shadow tones bleeding into the sky.

Note > This effect emulates the silk-stocking technique when it is applied only to the high contrast part of the split-grade printing technique made famous by Max Ferguson and digitally remastered in his book *Digital Darkroom Masterclass* (Focal Press).

8. Create a Copy Merged layer by going to the Select menu and choosing 'All'. Then from the Edit menu choose 'Copy Merged'. Again from the Edit menu choose 'Paste'. This copies all of the information from the visible layers and pastes it to a new layer. The keyboard shortcut for these three steps is to hold down the Ctrl+Alt+Shift keys and then type the letter E (sometimes referred to as 'Stamp Visible'). Drag this new merged layer to the top of the layers stack if it is not already there. Use the Highlight/Shadow adjustment feature (Enhance > Adjust Lighting Shadows/Highlights) to lighten the overly dark shadows (a result of the 'Multiply' blend mode). A setting of 25 to 40% is usually sufficient to rescue the shadow tones. An alternative to this approach of lightening the shadows is to use a Levels adjustment layer in screen mode. Move the Highlight Output slider in the bottom right-hand corner of the Levels dialog box to the left to restrict the lightening to predominantly the shadow tones.

9. Set the foreground colors in the Tools palette to their default black and white settings. Click on the Create Adjustment Layer icon in the Layers palette and choose 'Gradient Map' from the menu. Check the 'Dither' option and then click on the gradient in the Gradient Map dialog box to open the Gradient Editor dialog box.

Note > The gradient must start with black and end with white otherwise your image will not use the full dynamic range possible.

10. The Gradient Editor dialog box allows you to assign colors to shadows, midtones and highlights. Click underneath the gradient to create a new color stop. Slide it to a location that reads approximately 25% at the bottom of the dialog box. Click on the color swatch to open the Color Picker dialog box. Cool colors such as blue are often chosen to give character to shadow tones. Create another stop and move it to a location that reads approximately 75%. This time try choosing a bright warm color to contrast with the blue chosen previously.

Drag these color sliders and observe the changes that occur in your image. Create bright highlights with detail and deep shadows with detail for maximum tonal impact. Be careful not to move the color stops too close together as banding or 'posterization' will occur in the image. Choose desaturated colors from the Color Picker (less than 40%) to keep the effects reasonably subtle. Once you have created the perfect gradient you can give it a name and save it by clicking on the New button. This gradient will now appear in the gradient presets for quick access.

PERFORMANCE TIP

The gradient map used in this toning project uses a midtone color stop and can be downloaded from the supporting DVD and loaded directly from the Gradient Editor dialog box or by using the preset manager (go to 'Edit > Preset Manager > Gradients > Load'). Then browse to the Maximum_Performance.grd preset and select OK. Quick split-tone effects can be accessed via the Maximum Performance split- tone actions available on the DVD.

Experiment with lowering the opacity of the Gradient Map layer to allow some of the underlying color to blend with the colors introduced with the Gradient Map toning technique.

11. The final image is lightened by stamping all of the visible elements to a new layer (Ctrl+Alt+Shift and then type the letter E) and switching the blend mode to 'Screen'. A vignette in Overlay mode can be added to further increase the drama. An elliptical selection was feathered by 150 pixels and the selection inverted (Select > Inverse). The Selection has been filled with black and the opacity of the layer lowered to 60%.

12. The saturation in the corners of the image will have increased due to the 'Overlay' blend mode used in the previous step. To reduce this saturation Ctrl+click the vignette layer to pick up the selection of the ellipse and then use a Hue/Saturation adjustment layer. Finish off your toning project by stamping the visible elements to a new layer and apply the Unsharp Mask or Adjust Sharpness.

Project 5

Character Portrait

It is often possible to unleash the hidden potential of an image without going to the hassle of making fiddly selections. This project demonstrates how the tonality of an image can be enriched using duplicated layers, blend modes and a couple of filters to shape and sharpen. Dust off your trophy shelf - I feel an award coming on!

The beauty of these techniques is that we can let Photoshop Elements do all of the hard work and extract an image that has all of the hallmarks of a professionally lit studio-quality portrait from an image illuminated with nothing more than ambient light. The secret to success, if you plan to reuse this recipe on one of your own images, is to start with a razor sharp image illuminated by soft directional light (diffused window light is ideal).

DVD

16 BITS/CHANNEL IMAGE
ON SUPPORTING DVD

Cooking up some character - a recipe for success

Preparing the image

Before we start our culinary masterpiece we should prepare the main ingredient - the image. This should include optimizing the histogram via a manual or auto Levels adjustment (if you have the luxury of accessing a 16 Bit/Channel file via a RAW capture or a 48-bit scan your histogram will appreciate the Levels adjustment prior to hitting the '8 Bits/Channel' option in the Image > Mode submenu). Start the project by removing any distractions in the image so that the viewer's focus will not wander from the *pièce de résistance* - the face containing the character and majesty of our sitter. Keeping it simple is a key to clean and effective design.

1. You can either paint directly on to the background layer or duplicate the layer if you want to preserve the background layer unadjusted. Remember you have the option to undo any brush stroke that is not absolutely effective. In fact Elements allows you to undo 50 steps by default. Check the preferences and adjust the number to suit your own workflow if required. I think 50 is overly generous and this can consume excessive portions of the computer's available RAM that would be best served being made available for the more memory-intensive editing tasks we are about to engage in. There is no need to restart the computer if you decide to lower the number of 'History States' to 20 or even 10.

Dodge tool > Use a soft edged brush and paint with the Dodge tool set to 'Highlights'. Reduce the opacity to around 20 to 30% to ensure that you lighten the background in the top left-hand corner without unduly affecting the sitter's hat. Lower the opacity to 10% to lighten the rest of the background on this side (around the beard). The following steps will ensure that this backdrop will look like something from a studio (rather than the bus shelter where this image was captured).

Burn tool > Use a similar soft edged brush and paint with the Burn tool set to 'Midtones' to reduce the distracting pattern of the clothing. You are not aiming to remove the texture - just subdue it.

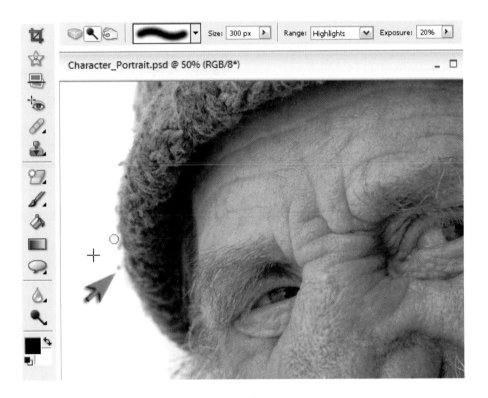

Spot Healing Brush > The Healing Brush tool is the best tool for removing distracting details or dust marks. Use a hard edged Healing Brush when working in areas of large tonal difference, e.g. removing the dark woollen bobbles that are surrounded by the white background. This will ensure the healing area is not contaminated with the adjacent tones of the nearby hat.

2. To start working on the tonality we need to separate the 'luminance' or brightness values from the color component of the image. Start the process by dragging the background layer to the New Layer icon in the Tools palette to duplicate it (alternatively use the keyboard shortcut Ctrl+J on a PC). From the Enhance menu choose the Remove Color command from the Adjust Color submenu. This will create a desaturated layer sitting above the colored background layer.

3. The fine detail of this portrait is going to be more pronounced if we create some smooth underlying tones. These smooth tones will also help to increase the three-dimensional quality of the portrait. Duplicate the desaturated layer using the same technique used in the previous step and then go to the Filter menu and choose 'Gaussian Blur' from the Blur submenu. Choose a generous Radius value - one where the skin tones are very smooth but the facial features can still be made out. When the 'Blur Radius' is selected choose OK.

4. Switch the blend mode of the blurred layer to 'Multiply'. The Multiply mode blends the blurred tones back into the sharp detail underneath but renders the image temporarily dark. The shadow information, although very dark, is not lost or 'clipped' by this blending technique. The overall brightness of this image will be restored in the next step so that we can appreciate how effective this technique has been.

Multiply mode > The 'Multiply' blend mode is one of the most useful blend modes for creative editing of digital images. The 'Multiply' blend mode belongs to the 'Darken' family grouping. The brightness values of the pixels on the blend layer and underlying layer are multiplied to create darker tones. Only values that are multiplied with white (level 255) stay the same.

PERFORMANCE TIP

One of the really essential techniques for multilayered image editing is the ability to take all of the combined elements from the visible layers and stamp them to a single new layer. It is so important that Adobe have decided to keep the shortcut a secret. The long way to achieve this stamping process involves choosing 'Select All' from the Select menu, choosing 'Copy Merged' from the Edit menu and then choosing 'Paste', again from the Edit menu.

Stamp Visible – the mother of all keyboard shortcuts

The shortcut is long, very long, but will save you considerable time as this technique is used over and over again in this style of editing. It will also impress the socks off image editors who are self-taught and who are most unlikely to have come across this permutation as it involves holding down nearly all of the left side of the keyboard! Hold down the Ctrl, Alt and Shift modifier keys and then (whilst still holding down the modifier keys) press the letters N followed by the letter E. If your new layer is not on top of the layers stack click and drag it to the top of the Layers palette.

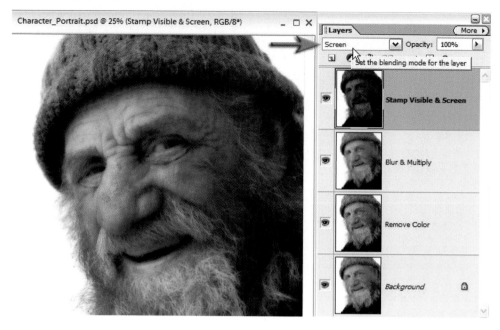

5. To restore the majority of the brightness values to this image simply switch the blending mode of this layer to 'Screen'. The 'Screen' blend mode belongs to the 'Lighten' family grouping and has the opposite effect to the 'Multiply' blend mode. The action of first multiplying and then dividing (screening) has however incorporated the blur layer into the pixel stew and the visual outcome is altogether different from the start image.

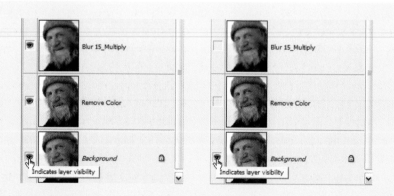

PERFORMANCE TIP

When working on a long project it is often necessary, or reassuring, to perform a quick taste test, i.e. gain a quick reminder of how life started out for this image and whether the techniques you are using are creating positive or negative visual outcomes. Rather than clicking on each Eye icon, on each individual layer, to switch the visibility off (one by one) you can simplify the process by simply holding down the Alt key and clicking only the Eye icon on the background layer. This action switches all of the other layers off in a single click, enabling you to see how life for this image started out. Alt+Click a second time to switch all of the layers back on. Looking good? Then let's proceed.

6. Sometimes tones need to be rescued if they are getting too close to 0 or 255. As the shadows are starting to make friends with level 0 and getting a little too close for comfort we must instigate a rescue attempt. We will need to merge all of the visible elements again (as in step 4) to a new layer (Stamp Visible) if we are to utilize our good friend and ally - Shadows/Highlights.

The Shadows/Highlights adjustment feature is an excellent tool for targeting shadow or highlight tones that need to be massaged in isolation and brought back into the range of tones that can be comfortably printed using an inkjet printer. Although the 'Screen' blend mode did an excellent job of moving the midtones and highlight tones back to their former glory, the shadows of this image are still struggling to emerge above a level where they are likely to print with detail (between level 10 and level 20 depending on the type of paper, ink and printer being used). The adjustment feature can be accessed via the Enhance > Lighting menu. Before accessing the adjustment feature it is probably worth having either the Histogram palette or the Info palette open so that you can gauge when the shadows have been restored to a value that will print on your trusty inkjet printer. Raising the Midtone Contrast slider can also inject some life and drama into the tonality of the image. You may need to do a balancing act between the two sliders whilst observing the numerical or visual effects to your tonal range if you intend to make use of the Midtone Contrast slider.

PERFORMANCE TIP

Shadows/ Highlights > The Shadows/ Highlights adjustment feature is the most sophisticated tool for lowering excessive contrast in Adobe Elements. The tool made a very welcome appearance in Elements 3.0 and forms part of the sophisticated armory of adjustment features that can enable users to edit the tonal qualities of an image with control and confidence in a non-destructive way (this armory of course does NOT include the Brightness/Contrast adjustment feature which serves no useful purpose and should be assigned to the wastelands of oblivion).

7. The next step involves getting rid of the distracting white background and replacing it with something a little more dramatic. Before creating a gradient make sure that black is the foreground color in the Tools palette (type D on the keyboard to return the color swatches to their default setting). From the Create adjustment layer menu in the Layers palette choose 'Gradient'. The creation of a radial gradient or 'vignette' involves fours steps. First choose the 'Radial', 'Reverse' and 'Dither' options in the Gradient Fill dialog box and enter a value of 150% in the 'Scale' field and then choose an appropriate angle (I have followed the angle of the face). The second step involves clicking on the gradient to open the Gradient Editor. Choose the 'Foreground to Transparent' preset and move the opacity stop on the far right of the gradient ramp to the left to clear the face of any tone, thereby pushing the starting point of the gradient to the edge of the face. For the third step select OK to close the Gradient Editor and then drag inside the image window to move the center of the gradient to the perfect position. Finally (step 4) select OK and adjust the opacity of the layer to balance the background tone with the portrait.

PERFORMANCE TIP
Gradient layers > One feature short of a full load

Although gradient layers represent an important and powerful editing tool, the good people at Adobe overlooked a very important aspect in this adjustment layer feature. Gradients have a nasty habit of 'banding', either in the screen view and/or in the printed image, giving the tonal transition a posterized appearance that is not at all in keeping with the rich tonal qualities of advanced image-editing techniques. The banding can only partly be reduced by selecting the 'Dither' option (not a default option for the gradients). To ensure this banding does not raise its ugly head the user must add noise to any areas of smooth tone after any gradients have been applied. Gradient layers unfortunately do not contain pixels to which noise can be added so this can become especially problematic and requires an additional noise layer to resolve the problem.

8. Adding noise rather than reducing noise may sound strange. One has to remember however that the gradient is completely artificial and completely noiseless - something that cannot be matched even with a low-noise image captured on a digital camera using a low ISO setting. By adding noise we are merely trying to match the noise present in the rest of the image and at the same time eliminate or reduce the problem of banding. To create a Noise layer hold down the Alt key and click on the New Layer icon in the Layers palette. In the New Layer dialog box choose 'Overlay' as the mode and click on the 'Fill with Overlay-neutral color (50% gray)' checkbox.

Select OK and then switch off the visibility of the Gradient layer so that we can see the original white background. Only one selection is used in this project and it is used to isolate the background for the noise treatment. Select the 'Magic Wand' from the Tools palette and select the 'Sample all layers' option in the Options bar. Deselect the 'Contiguous' box and lower the tolerance to 20 to ensure that the selection is painless - a single click should do the trick. You will need to add a generous amount of feather (100 pixels or more) to this mask to create a gradual transition between noise and no noise (Select > Feather). After feathering the selection switch the visibility of the gray overlay layer back on. Zoom in to 100 or 200% (avoid magnifications that do not give an accurate screen view, e.g. 133% etc.).

9. With the selection still active select the Add Noise filter from the Filter > Noise submenu. Select the 'Monochromatic' option and choose an amount that will create a noise level that is consistent with the rest of the image file. To check that the noise level is OK hold down the spacebar to enable you to drag the image between the gradient (with added noise) and the face (with no added noise). When the texture is consistent select OK.

Note > Adding noise is an essential component of using gradients. Think gradient - think noise.

10. The localized contrast is already vastly improved from the original file but if you want to see how far you can take this tonal manipulation you may like to try the following technique that can add depth and volume to a seemingly lifeless and flat image. Stamp the visible elements yet again to another new layer (Ctrl+Alt+Shift and then type E) and then switch the blend mode to 'Overlay'. From the Filter menu go to the Other submenu and choose the High Pass filter. When this filter is used as an alternative to the Unsharp Mask filter a small radius of between 1 and 5 is usually selected, depending on the resolution of the image file and the output medium, but in this case the Radius slider can be moved to a much higher radius whilst observing the effects to the image file. At the moment the effects may appear a little excessive but lowering the opacity of the layer and/or switching the blend mode of the layer to 'Soft Light' can refine the overall effect.

11. The rich tonality will now serve as an excellent canvas for the fine detail that we are about to sharpen. Sharpening should always appear late in the editing process to avoid exaggerating any image artifacts or non-image data. If you are to have maximum control over the sharpening process and the flexibility to adjust the level of sharpening after making a test print (images tend to look a little softer when compared to their screen counterpart - especially when using TFT displays), you need to apply the Unsharp Mask to a Copy Merged layer. You know the drill by now - stamp visible to a new layer. When this has been done you should set the blend mode to 'Luminosity'. Switching the layer to the 'Luminosity' blend mode will have zero effect on the visual outcome of the image at this stage. The advantage of this mode change is when the color is switched back on in the next and final step of the project. If you are used to applying conservative values in the Unsharp Mask filter this is not the time to exercise constraint. Be generous - very generous - with the Amount slider (200 in this project) but keep the Radius slider to the usual amount (no more than 1.5). The Threshold slider, which is usually raised to avoid sharpening minor details, can either be left at 0 so that all of the image information comes under the global sharpening umbrella or raised to around 5 so that the image noise levels are not excessively sharpened. You will need to print a test strip to your favorite paper surface before you can assess whether the amount of sharpening for this image is correct. If the sharpening seems a little excessive simply lower the opacity of the sharpening layer until you find the perfect setting for your paper.

12. You might be so impressed with the tonal qualities of your monochrome masterpiece that the thought of switching the color back on gives you the shivers. It is important, however, to the learning curve of this project, to discover how the luminance values of an image file can be edited independently of the color before being reunited. Color can be a major distraction when editing tonality. Switching off the visibility of the three monochrome or desaturated layers sitting directly above the background layer will allow the top layer in Luminosity mode to merge with the color of the background layer. The blend modes are one of the most underutilized of the editing features to be found in Photoshop Elements. Perhaps it is because of their slightly abstract names and their mathematical approach to multilayered pixel editing but their creative power and usefulness should not be underestimated. With the digitally remastered dish ready to serve up to your printer you may need to savor both monochrome and color versions over a period of time before your own personal preference helps you make the final decision. Enjoy!

MULTILAYERED PSD
ON SUPPORTING DVD

Color is fed back into the character portrait image to create the above effect

Project 6

Maximum Performance

Use the soft focus action to achieve a lightening fast makeover (minus the heal and liquify steps)

Glamor Portrait

Cheaper (and more fun) than plastic surgery we explore how pixel surgery can be used to craft perfect portraits that are bound to flatter the sitter every time.

The glamor portrait offers an excellent opportunity to test the effectiveness of a variety of image-editing skills. The portrait is an unforgiving canvas that will show any heavy-handed or poor technique that may be applied. We will start with a color portrait that has been captured using a soft diffused light source.

This project will aim to perfect various features and not to make such changes that the character of the sitter is lost to the technique. The techniques used do not excessively smooth or obliterate the skin texture that would, in turn, lead to an artificial or plastic appearance. The techniques used smooth imperfections without totally eliminating them.

DVD

16 BITS/CHANNEL IMAGE
ON SUPPORTING DVD

The 15-minute (after practice) makeover - techniques designed to flatter your model

PERFORMANCE TIP

Use window light or diffused flash to obtain a soft low-contrast light source to flatter the subject. Avoid direct flash unless it is diffused with a white umbrella. Stand back from your sitter and zoom in with your lens rather than coming in close and distorting the features of the face (the closer you stand - the bigger the nose of the sitter appears). A perfect white background is difficult to create if you don't have a studio backdrop and multiple lights but, with a little practice, it is possible to get a near white background by capturing the sitter in front of a white translucent curtain against a brightly illuminated window and with a single introduced light source.

1. If you can capture using the RAW format then you will have the opportunity of perfecting the histogram and color balance in 16 Bits/Channel mode prior to starting the project. Drag the Shadow and Highlight sliders in to meet the histogram or simply click the Auto button. Drop the bit depth once this has been done to 8-bit mode (Image > Mode > 8 Bits/Channel).

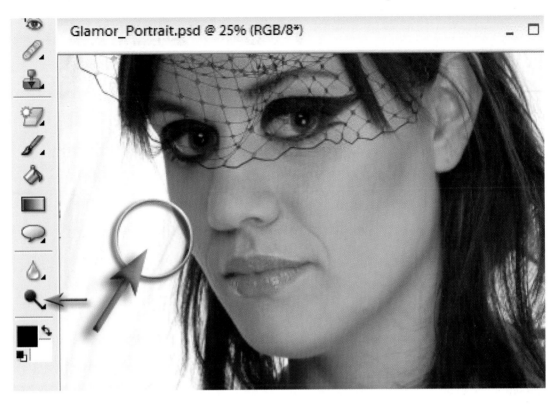

2. Select the 'Dodge tool' in the Tools palette and in the Options bar choose 'Highlights' and an exposure setting of a round 20 to 30%. If you are a little nervous about using this tool on the background layer duplicate the background layer by dragging it to the New Layer icon in the Layers palette. Stroke the background with a large soft brush until any detail or tone present is rendered white. As the Dodge tool in Highlight mode only lightens the brightest tones on the layer, care only needs to be taken if the skin tones or hair next to the white background are also very bright.

3. As you move through this project it is worth saving consecutive versions. The Organizer in Elements can keep track of these versions and help name them if you click on the 'Save in Version Set with Original' option when you first use the Save As command from the File menu.

4. A timesaving technique when working with the Healing Brush tool is to either duplicate the background layer or create a new empty layer before starting the healing process. You can simply fade all of your work at the end of the process by dropping the opacity of the healing layer. If you choose to heal to an empty layer make sure that this is the layer that is selected in the Layers palette and the 'Sample All Layers' option is selected in the Options bar.

PERFORMANCE TIP

Care must be taken when selecting the size and hardness of the brush. If an overly large soft edged brush is used near the eyes, lips or hair it can draw in color values that can contaminate the skin tones (a selection can be made prior to using the Healing Brush to isolate the healing area from different colors or tones). If the brush is too hard the edges of the healing area will be visible. Sometimes it is better to use a smaller brush and make several passes rather than trying to complete the section with a single pass. The Healing Brush tool, with its protection of surface texture, is a superior alternative to using the Rubber Stamp tool at a reduced opacity.

Project 6: Glamor Portrait

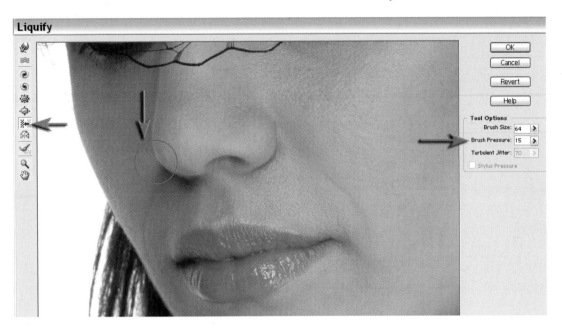

5. The Liquify filter is another tool that works directly on your pixels so you may like to duplicate the Background layer if you are feeling nervous about the pixel surgery that follows. The various tools in the Liquify filter dialog box can be used to modify the shape or size of the sitter's features. The Pucker tool and Bloat tool can be used to contract or expand various features, e.g. grow eyes or lips and shrink noses. Perhaps the most useful of the Liquify tools however is the Shift Pixels tool. This tool can be used to move pixels to the left when stroking down and to the right when stroking up. This tool is ideal for trimming off unsightly fat or reshaping features. In this project the brush pressure is dropped to 15% and an appropriate brush size is selected so that the side of the face is not moved along with the nose. If things start to get ugly just remember the keyboard shortcut Ctrl+Z (undo)!

Note > It is important to exercise great restraint when using the Liquify filter, as the face can quickly become a cartoon caricature of itself when taken too far. The filter also softens detail that becomes obvious when overdone.

PERFORMANCE TIP

It is possible to 'freeze' pixels to protect them from the actions of the Liquify filter. There is a freeze brush in the Liquify filter of the full version of Photoshop - but not so in Elements. To activate the freeze in Elements simply make a feathered selection prior to selecting the Liquify filter. Select the area to be modified, being careful to leave out sections of the face that should be protected from the pixel surgery. With the selection active open the Liquify dialog box. The areas outside of the selection are now frozen.

6. Create a Hue/Saturation adjustment layer. Focus your attention on the whites of the eyes and lower the saturation until any discoloring in the eyes is removed. Disregard the effects to the rest of the face for the time being. Select OK and then fill the layer mask with black to conceal the adjustment (Alt+Backspace if black is in the foreground color swatch or Ctrl+Backspace if black is in the background color swatch).

Select the 'Brush tool' from the Tools palette. Choose a soft edged brush just a little smaller than the eye in the Options bar and lower the opacity to 50%. Choose white as the foreground color in the Tools palette. Stroke the eyes with the brush until the whites are appropriately drained of color.

7. Create a Levels adjustment layer and move the Gamma slider to the left to brighten the whites of the eyes. As before select OK and then fill the layer mask with black to conceal the adjustment once again.

This time brighten the eyes by painting with white at 50% opacity. If you overdo it you can switch colors and paint with black or simply lower the opacity of the adjustment layer.

8. This technique is fast and effective. The first step is to merge all of the visible elements of this image into a new layer on top of the layers stack (referred to as 'Stamp Visible'). Hold down all of the modifier keys (the Ctrl, Shift and Alt keys) and then type in the letter E (on Version 3 you will need to type in the letter N followed by the letter E). Make sure the resulting layer is on top of the layers stack and set the blend mode of this layer to 'Multiply'. Go to the Filter menu and choose 'Gaussian Blur' from the Blur submenu. Apply a 20-pixel Gaussian Blur.

Visual warning > Now it is going to look like someone turned out some of the lights until we carry out the next stage of the process, but if you use your imagination you can probably already see that the skin tones are now smooth and radiant - if just a tad dark.

PERFORMANCE TIP

The precise pixel radius of the Gaussian Blur filter will vary depending on the resolution of your image. The idea is to bleed the tones, but not so much as to lose the features of the face. Reduce the size of the preview in the Filter dialog box to gain an idea of the extent of the blur on this layer. Back off before you start losing features of the face.

9. Use the same monster keyboard shortcut as in step 8 to 'stamp' the visible elements to a new layer. Set the blend mode of this layer to Screen mode to lighten the image. If the image is still not light enough you will need to drag this layer to the New Layer icon to duplicate it. The blend mode of this duplicate layer will also be in Screen mode. If this lightens the image too much simply lower the opacity of this layer until you strike the correct balance.

10. Create a Hue/Saturation layer above these screened layers and lower the saturation a little. The side effect to smoothing the skin tones using this technique is that saturation increases. Another problem that will need to be resolved is that the deepest shadow tones may be pushed too dark to print. These important shadow tones will need to be rescued in order to produce a professional result.

Fine-tuning the tonality

11. There are a number of different ways we can rescue the shadow tones of this image. The first technique uses the non-destructive dodge layer technique. Hold down the Alt key whilst you click on the New Layer icon in the Layers palette. Switch the mode to 'Overlay' and check the 'Fill with Overlay-neutral color (50% gray)' box. Select OK. This 50% gray layer is invisible in 'Overlay' mode but can be used to lighten or darken the underlying image.

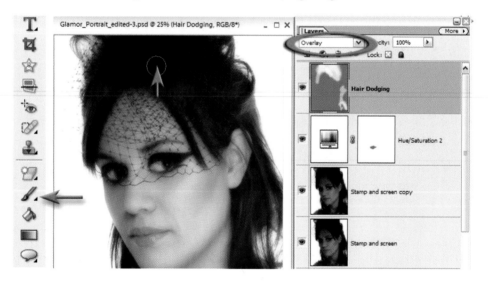

Select 'White' as the foreground color and use a soft edged brush at 50% opacity to paint the darkest areas of the hair lighter. Several passes at a reduced opacity rather than a single pass at 100% opacity will render the dodging a subtle affair.

> PERFORMANCE TIP
>
> If you require more 'oomph' to your dodging, or less saturation with your burning, try switching the blend mode of your dodge and burn layer to Soft Light mode instead of Overlay mode.

12. The Shadows/Highlights adjustment feature from the Enhance > Adjust Lighting submenu can also be used to target and rescue the darker tones of your image. Stamp Visible to a new layer before implementing the adjustment. When using a layer mask with the Shadows/Highlights adjustment command it is possible to pump up the level of lightening and midtone contrast without affecting the midtones or highlights in the image.

PERFORMANCE TIP

The Shadows/Highlights is a very powerful adjustment feature. Use a layer mask to further limit or restrict the effects of the Shadows/Highlights adjustment. Create a Levels adjustment layer without making any adjustment (simply click OK). Copy the image to the clipboard (Edit > Copy Merged) and paste it into the layer mask of this adjustment layer. In order to paste the image into the layer mask you must first Alt+Click the layer mask. When you Alt+Click an empty layer mask the image window will appear completely white. From the Edit menu choose 'Paste'. If this action is not taken the copied pixels will be pasted to a new layer. To restrict the adjustment to just the darkest tones of the image you must first invert the image in the layer mask (Ctrl+I) and then perform a Levels adjustment (Ctrl+L) to this layer mask. Move the Shadow slider to the right to restrict the lightening process to just the darkest shadows. Move the Highlight slider to the left to increase the effect of the Shadows adjustment.

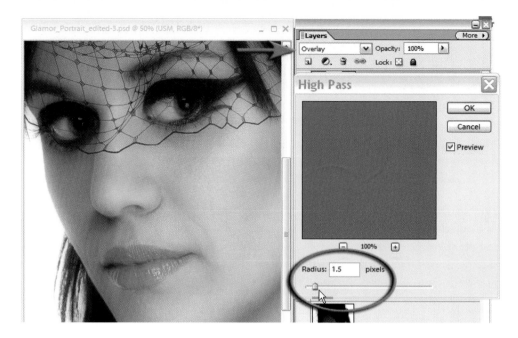

13. Smooth skin tones can be unduly sensitive to the application of the Unsharp Mask. It is usual to raise the Threshold slider sufficiently so that areas of smooth tonal gradation are left unaffected. Film grain, image sensor noise and minor skin defects all come in for the sharpening treatment if the threshold is left too low. If the sharpening process is proving problematic using the Unsharp Mask a selective sharpening technique should be considered. Stamp Visible to a new layer, set the blend mode to 'Overlay' and apply the High Pass filter (Filter > Other > High Pass). At this stage the sharpening is global but it can be restricted by using a layer mask borrowed from an adjustment layer or by painting directly into this High Pass layer using 50% gray to eliminate sharpening.

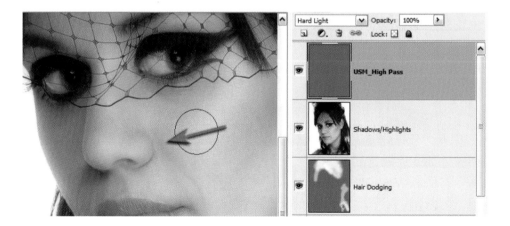

Click on a 50% gray swatch in the Swatches palette or click on the foreground color swatch in the Tools palette and set the HSB values to 0, 0 and 50. With 50% gray as your foreground color you can now proceed to paint the smoother areas of skin to ensure they escape the sharpening process.

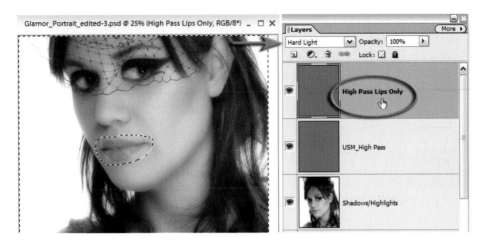

14. You can add a little lip-gloss (or extra sparkle to the eyes) by duplicating the High Pass layer and filling the rest of the image with 50% gray. Make selections of the lips and/or eyes and then invert the selection. Then choose 'Fill Selection' from the Edit menu and choose 50% gray. Switching the mode of the layer to 'Hard Light' will pump up the effect to maximum.

It might seem like a long road to the final result but this technique can be surprisingly quick when you get into the swing of things. It avoids excessive selections and fiddly work, and a lot of minor blemishes are nuked via the blurred layer set to Multiply mode. Of course the real reward will be the admiration of your photographic skills by the sitter - who will be eternally grateful.

PERFORMANCE TIP

If you can't leave well enough alone, or would just like to explore different approaches to the make-up the model is using, then you can add your own make-up in post-production instead of pre-production. Add a new empty layer set to Multiply mode. Using a soft paint brush set to 50% opacity build up some eye shadow, rouge or lipstick and then lower the opacity of the layer until you create the right effect.

Try grouping a Hue/Saturation slider with the make-up layer and move the Hue and Saturation slider to explore alternative shades quickly and easily. If only getting ready to go out for the evening was this simple!

DVD
IMAGE ON DVD

Create this image using techniques from Project 1 in this section of the book - image by Dorothy Connop

Project 7

Motion Blur

If you have a need for speed and would like to 'move it, move it' this project shows you how to get some ooomph into your stationary wagon.

To get some motion magic happening we need to start with nothing more than a half decent parked car. The example used in this project may look like your professional car shoot but was in fact captured using a fixed lens digicam in a school car park. With little more than a selection, a couple of blur filters and a little know-how the static becomes dramatic.

A 1999 Corvette is polished and taken for a spin in this classic car makeover

The post-production editing or 'car makeover' is simplified when there are not too many reflections in the bodywork or chrome of the car that you capture. Busy reflections will either detract from the final quality or increase the time you spend removing the unwanted detail. In this tutorial you will learn how to smooth out the bodywork, streak the background and spin the wheels, and finally put the icing on the corporate cake by applying the logos to give the image that advertising look.

Stage 1 - Cleaning the paintwork

1. If you are not experienced using the Healing Brush tool and Clone Stamp tool I would recommend duplicating the background layer by dragging it to the New Layer icon in the Layers palette. This will give you the option of trashing the layer if all goes horribly wrong. Hold down the Alt key and click on an area of good paintwork and then paint over any scratches, blemishes or damaged areas. Vary both the size and the hardness of the brush to get the best results. If you are working in the middle of a panel the Healing Brush tool usually gives the best results. If you are working close to an edge you may want to try increasing the hardness of the brush in the Options bar or switching to the Clone Stamp tool. Double-click on the layer name in the Layers palette and name it 'Clean' to differentiate it from the background layer.

2. Make a selection of the car using one of the tools from the Lasso group. The Magnetic Lasso tool will do a good job of selecting most of the car. Select only the car, excluding its shadow. Click on an edge of the car with the Magnetic Lasso tool and move the tool slowly along the edge to start the process. You will notice that the tool lays down anchor points. When moving the tool over an edge with poor contrast you can help Photoshop along a little by pressing the shift key and clicking to add an anchor point manually (Photoshop cannot see some edges due to the poor contrast). Alternatively you can fine-tune the sensitivity of the tool by experimenting with the settings in the Options bar. From the Select menu choose 'Save Selection', give your selection a name such as 'Car' and click OK.

3. The next part of the process involves separating the edges of the car from the broader areas of paintwork. This will allow us to smooth out the paintwork whilst retaining the definition and detail of the edges. Duplicate the layer you have just cleaned and healed (if you duplicated the background layer in the first step you will now have three layers in your layers palette) and apply a 1-pixel Gaussian Blur (Filter > Blur > Gaussian Blur). This prepares the file for the filter used in the next step.

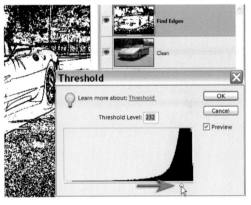

4. Choose the Find Edges filter found in the Stylize submenu (Filter > Stylize > Find Edges) to reduce this layer to the edges only. To increase the contrast and width of the edges we can apply the Threshold filter from the Adjustments submenu (Filter > Adjustments > Threshold). Drag the slider in the Threshold dialog box to the right until you have well-defined black lines and limited detail visible in the panels. Name the layer you have been working on to save any possible confusion later. I have called mine 'Find Edges'.

5. Select the 'Brush tool' in the Tools palette and 'White' as the foreground color (press the letter D on your keyboard to set the colors to their default settings and then press the letter X to switch the foreground and background colors). Paint to remove any detail in the paintwork that is not required, i.e. anything that is not the edge of a panel or important detail that needs to be pin sharp. Load the selection (Select > Load Selection) that you saved earlier in step 2. Check the Invert box and then select OK. The background should now be selected.

6. Choose 'Fill Selection' from the Edit menu and select 'Black' for the contents color. Select OK. Your image should now appear as a line drawing of the car with a black background. Choose 'Deselect' from the Select menu.

146

7. To soften the lines so that detail of the edges fades gradually into the smooth paintwork we must apply a small amount of Gaussian Blur to this layer. Although softening the edges the Gaussian Blur may also reduce the density of the lines, so follow the Gaussian Blur with a Levels adjustment (Enhance > Adjust Lighting > Levels). In the Levels dialog box move the central Gamma slider underneath the histogram to the right until the lines once again appear black. This is now the resource for our mask that we will use to protect the important detail when we smooth out the superfluous detail in the bodywork.

8. To transfer this layer to a mask we need to choose 'All' from the Select menu. Photoshop Elements cannot add a layer mask to a pixel layer so we will need to borrow a mask from an adjustment layer. Create a Levels adjustment layer and then select OK without making any adjustment. Hold down the Alt key and click on the layer mask of this adjustment layer in the Layers palette. The image window will appear white (you are now viewing the contents of the layer mask, and as yet there is nothing in there). Now choose 'Paste' from the Edit menu and the line drawing of your car should now appear. Alt-click the layer mask a second time and choose 'Deselect' from the Select menu. Although it appears you are still viewing the layer mask you are in fact viewing the layer beneath which is identical.

9. Click on the Eye icon to hide the visibility of the mask resource layer I have called 'Find Edges' (the one below the adjustment layer) or discard it by dragging it to the Trashcan icon in the Layers palette. Create a duplicate of the layer that you cleaned in step 1 by holding down the Alt key and dragging it to the top of the layers stack. Group this layer with the adjustment layer supporting your layer mask by going to the Layer menu and choosing the command Group with Previous.

10. Apply a small amount of Gaussian Blur to this Clean Copy layer - 1 or 2 pixels is usually required if you are using a file from a fixed lens digital compact or prosumer camera. This step will create smooth paintwork by removing superfluous detail and image noise. The important detail such as the crisp edges to the bodywork and panels will not be affected due to the actions of the mask below. If you have used more than 1-pixel Gaussian Blur to smooth the paintwork you may need to add 1% noise to this layer to prevent possible tonal banding or posterization (visual steps of tone instead of a smooth transition of tone).

Stage 2 – Blurring the background

11. Now that the car looks brand new we can add the dramatic element in this project. Load the selection of your car ensuring the Invert box is checked again (Select > Load Selection). Create another adjustment layer with the selection still active. There is no need to make any adjustment. We are again just using the adjustment layer to access its layer mask. The active selection will create its own layer mask. Again whilst holding down the Alt key drag a copy of the clean layer to the top of the layers stack. You may want to rename your previous clean copy layer to save any possible confusion or to remember any settings you have used.

12. Before we apply the Motion Blur filter to this copy layer we must prepare the layer so that the car is not streaked into the background, thereby creating a ghost image of itself. Select the 'Clone Stamp tool' from the Tools palette. Choose a large soft edged brush set to 100% opacity in the Options bar. Clone away the front and the rear of the car by setting a source point in the road in the lower right-hand corner of the image. To set the source point hold down the Alt key and click your mouse. Clone away the top of the car by moving the source point to the trees above the windscreen. There is no need to be overly precise with this work, as any imperfections will be hidden when the Motion Blur filter is applied in the next step.

Important > Do not clone away any of the shadow of the car.

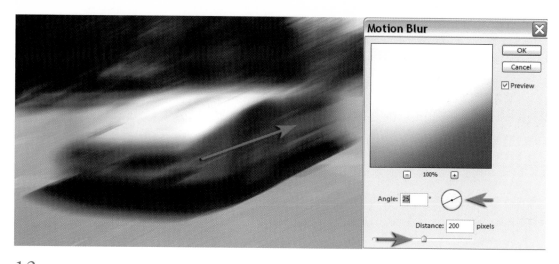

13. Go to the Filter menu and choose 'Motion Blur' from the Blur submenu. Drag the Distance slider to the right to increase the apparent speed of the car. Adjust the angle using the little wheel or by entering a figure in the field so that the streaked lines of the blurred background appear to line up with the angle of the car and then select OK. Group the motion blur layer with the adjustment layer beneath by choosing the Group with Previous command from the Layer menu. Although we now have an impressive result the image is not yet perfect.

14. We must now turn our attentions to the shadows. The Motion Blur filter may drag lighter tones underneath where the wheels make contact with the ground. This will give the illusion that the car is floating above the road instead of in contact with it. To darken the road immediately next to the tires we can use an adjustment layer. To prevent the adjustment layer from lightening the entire image we simply need to add the adjustment layer to the group. Hold down the Alt key as you click on the Adjustment Layer icon in the Layers palette and select a Levels adjustment layer. When the New Layer dialog box opens check the Group With Previous Layer box and select OK. When the Levels dialog box opens move the central Gamma slider underneath the histogram to the right to darken the road. Pay particular attention to the road directly in front of the rear wheel. Select OK when the tones match. To restrict this darkening process to just a small area around the wheels we must fill the layer mask with black. Go to the Edit menu and choose 'Fill Layer'. Select 'Black' as the contents and select OK. The effects of the adjustment layer will momentarily disappear.

15. Now choose the 'Brush tool' in the Tools palette and select 'White' as the foreground color. Drop the opacity of the brush to 50% and paint where the road requires darkening. Make several strokes with the brush (letting go of the mouse clicker after each stroke) until the road is darkened sufficiently.

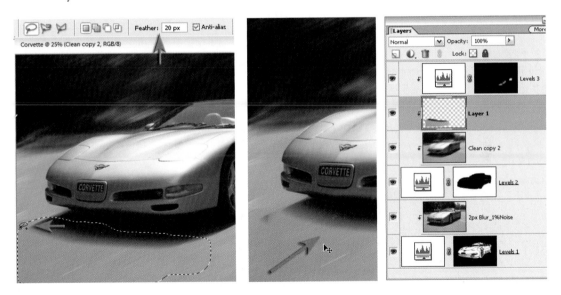

16. Make a selection using the Lasso tool using a 20-pixel feather. Select 'Copy' from the Edit menu and then select 'Paste' from the Edit menu. Group this layer with the Layer group underneath (Layer > Group with previous). Select the 'Move tool' and drag the shadow back underneath the car. Ignore the original shadow that may appear to the left, as this will be removed in the next step.

17. To remove any evidence of the original shadow select the 'Clone Stamp tool' and check the Sample All Layers box in the Options bar. This option will allow you to select the pixels from the layer underneath without first selecting it. Choose a sample point by holding down the Alt key and clicking the mouse. Now the Motion Blur will be convincing and the car will look like it is neither floating nor parked.

Stage 3 – Spinning the wheels

If you examine the pin-sharp wheels of the car you will probably appreciate that there is still more work to do before we can hide the fact that this car is actually static. We must apply a small amount of Motion Blur to the wheels but this needs to be a radial instead of linear Motion Blur.

18. Make a selection with the Circular Marquee tool using a 5-pixel feather. If you need to move the selection before it is complete (letting go of the mouse clicker will complete the selection) you can press the space bar and slide the selection to a better position. Copy the wheel using the Copy Merged command from the Edit menu. The Copy Merged command will copy all of the visible pixels instead of the pixels on the currently selected layer. Choose 'Paste' from the Edit menu to paste a copy of the wheel to a new layer.

Note > If the ellipse of the selection is slightly crooked when compared to the ellipse of the wheel that you are trying to select you can rotate the selection by using the Transform command (Image > Transform > Free Transform). You must however select an adjustment layer with an empty layer mask to ensure that no pixels are rotated when the elliptical selection is rotated. As none are currently available in this project you would have to create one.

Choose the Transform command (Image > Transform > Free Transform) and drag the side handle of the Bounding box until the wheel appears as a circle instead of an ellipse. To get the best result from the Radial Blur filter we must present the wheel on the same plane to the one in which the filter works, i.e. front on.

19. From the Blur group of Filters choose the Radial Blur filter. Check the radio buttons 'Spin' and 'Best' and start with a value of around 20 pixels before clicking OK. If the radial blue is excessive or insufficient choose 'Undo' from the Edit menu and then try the filter using an alternative amount. When you have applied the filter choose the Transform command again and return the wheel to its original elliptical shape. Repeat the process with the rear wheel.

Stage 4 – Adding the graphics

A classic car shot such as this would look great with a little window dressing. Rather than create the graphics from scratch a couple of extra close-up images were taken of the car model name and its distinctive logo of crossed flags.

20. Open the image 'Logo1' and then click and drag the background layer thumbnail in the Layers palette from this new image file into the window of the car image. Use the Move tool to drag it into position below the car. Set the layer to Luminosity mode in the Layers palette so the background behind the text adopts the same color as the road. You can create a softer edge to the background by using the rectangular Marquee tool and making a feathered selection around the name. I have used a 30-pixel feather in this project.

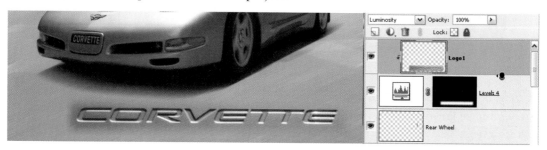

21. Select the layer beneath the Logo1 layer and then create a Levels adjustment layer (no adjustment required). The active selection will create a mask that we can use to soften the edge of the logo. To make use of this mask select the logo layer and then choose 'Group with Previous' from the Layer menu. We can disguise the tonal difference of the background by grouping a Levels adjustment layer with the logo layer (hold down the Alt key and check the option in the New Layer dialog box as in step 14).

22. Move the Gamma slider until the left side of the logo's background appears the same tone as the road (ignore the fact that the right side is now lighter than the road) and then select OK.

23. Select the 'Gradient tool' in the Tools palette and choose the 'Black', 'White gradient' and 'Linear' options in the Options bar. Click and drag a straight line from the end of the logo to the start of the logo (hold down the shift key whilst dragging your line to constrain the gradient to a straight line). This will shield the right side of the gradient from the excessive effects of the adjustment and create a tonal balance or uniformity along the width of the logo.

24. Open and drag in the second logo file. Use the Transform command to rescale the logo and move it into position. On the Artwork and Effects palette under Special Effects, choose the Layer Styles category and the Bevels subcategory, and apply the Simple Pillow Emboss style by double-clicking its icon in the palette. This will ensure the logo matches the style of the embossed letters. Delete the background surrounding this second logo if you wish to emboss only the flags instead of the entire layer.

Stage 5 – Completing the image

At last we are on the home straight. All we have to do is add a vignette to focus the attention on the car and then, as always, an appropriate amount of sharpening just prior to printing.

25. Create a new layer and make sure it is positioned above all other layers in the Layers palette. Choose the 'Circular Marquee tool' and select a 200-pixel Radius in the Options bar. Drag from the top left-hand corner of the image to the bottom right-hand corner of the image. Choose 'Inverse' from the Select menu and sample some of the dark green foliage using the Eyedropper tool. Then choose 'Fill Selection' from the Edit menu and select 'Foreground Color' as the contents. Drop the opacity of the vignette layer to create the right effect and use the Multiply mode for this layer if required.

26. Complete the project by sharpening the image. Select the top layer in the Layers palette and then hold down the Ctrl+Alt+Shift keys and type the letter N followed by the letter E. This keyboard shortcut will copy all of the visible layers and paste them to a new layer. Use a generous amount of sharpening (150 to 200) but keep the radius low (0.8 to 1.5). Threshold can be raised slightly (3 to 6) when using files from a digital compact rather than a digital SLR. Print the image to assess the appropriate amount of sharpening. If the sharpening is excessive lower the opacity of the unsharp mask layer. Perfection on a plate – well almost. For even more realism don't forget to add that quintessential ingredient that I missed in this project – the driver!

iStock_000001143384 (Endless Highway 2 by ra-photos)
iStock_000001300100 (BMW 318i by felixR)

PERFORMANCE TIP

When the movement is towards the camera the illusion of movement can be created by using the Radial Blur filter instead of the Motion Blur filter. To reduce the effects of the blur in the distance the filter can first be applied to a duplicate layer and this duplicate layer can then be grouped with an adjustment layer that contains a radial gradient. The sky was also masked using a linear gradient in Multiply mode.

The car in this illustration came from a separate image and was masked using techniques outlined in Project 1 of the Montage section (Part 3) in this book. The original shadow was preserved using the techniques outlined in Project 6 of the Montage section. The images used in this Performance Tip are courtesy of iStockphoto (www.iStockphoto.com) and are available for download from the supporting DVD.

Project 8

Low Key

A low-key image is where the dark tones dominate the photograph. Small bright highlights punctuate the shadow areas creating the characteristic mood of a low-key image. The position of the light source for a typical low-key image is behind the subject or behind and off to one side so that deep shadows are created. In the olden (pre-digital) days the appropriate exposure usually centred around how far the photographer could reduce the exposure before the highlights appeared dull. In the digital age this approach to exposure at the time of capture should be avoided at all costs, especially when black velvet-like tones are your benchmark for quality.

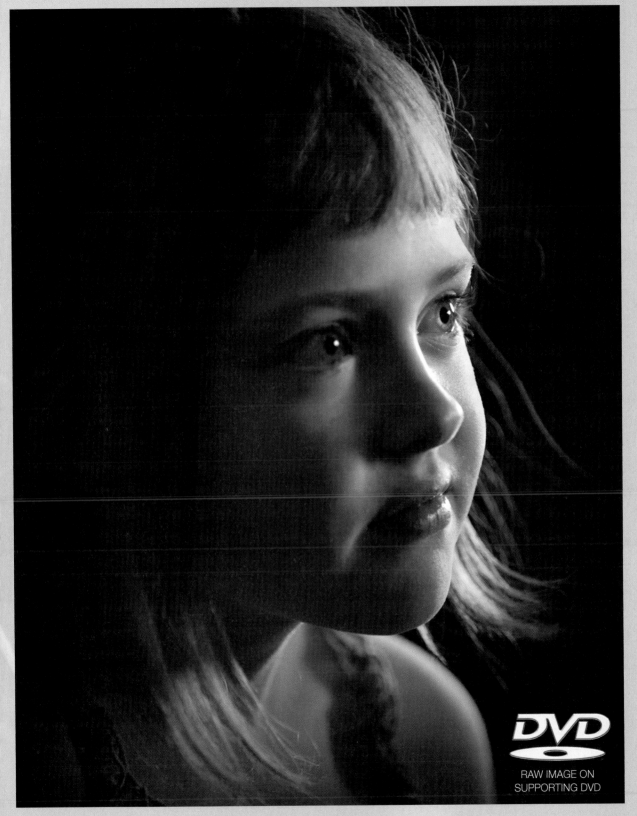

DVD
RAW IMAGE ON
SUPPORTING DVD

The classic low-key image - redefining exposure for a digital age

Exposure for low-key images

For those digital photographers interested in the dark side, an old SLR loaded with a fine-grain black and white film is a hard act to follow. The liquid smooth transitions and black velvet-like quality of dark low-key prints of yesteryear is something that digital capture is hard pressed to match. The sad reality of digital capture is that underexposure in low light produces noise and banding (steps rather than smooth transitions of tone) in abundance. The answer, however, is surprisingly simple for those who have access to a DSLR and have selected the RAW format from the Quality menu settings in their camera. The next step is to be generous with your exposure to the point of clipping or overexposing your highlights and only attempt to lower the exposure of the shadows in Adobe Camera RAW.

1. The first step is the most difficult to master for those who are used to using Auto or Program exposure modes. Although the final outcome may require deep shadow tones, the aim in digital low-key exposure is to first get the shadow tones away from the left-hand wall of the histogram by increasing and NOT decreasing the exposure. It is vitally important however not to increase the exposure so far that you lose or clip highlight detail. The original exposure of the image used in this project reveals that the shadow tones (visible as the highest peaks in the histogram) have had a generous exposure in-camera so that noise and banding have been avoided (the tones have moved well to the right in the histogram). The highlights however look as though they have become clipped or overexposed. The feedback from the histogram on the camera's LCD would have confirmed the clipping at the time of exposure (the tall peak on the extreme right-hand side of the histogram) and if you had your camera set to warn you of overexposure the highlights would have been merrily flashing at you to ridicule you of your sad attempts to expose this image. The typical DSLR camera is however a pessimist when it comes to clipped highlights and ignorant of what is possible in Adobe Camera RAW. Adobe Camera RAW can recover at least one stop of extra highlight information when the Exposure slider is dragged to the left (so long as the photographer has used a DSLR camera that has a broader dynamic range than your typical fixed lens compact digicam).

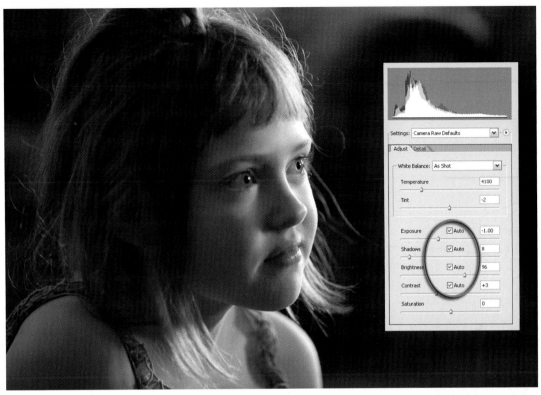

Adobe Camera RAW rescues the highlights – sometimes automatically

'Exposing right'

When the Auto checkbox in the Exposure slider is checked Adobe Camera RAW often attempts to rescue overexposed highlights automatically. With a little knowledge and some attention to the histogram during the capture stage you can master the art of pushing your highlights to the edge. So if your model is not in a hurry (mine is watching a half-hour TV show) you can take an initial exposure on Auto and then check your camera for overexposure. Increase the exposure using the exposure compensation dial on the camera until you see the flashing highlights. When the flashing highlights start to appear you can still add around one extra stop to the exposure before the highlights can no longer be recovered in Adobe Camera RAW. The popular term for this peculiar behavior is called 'exposing right'.

PERFORMANCE TIP

If the highlights are merrily flashing and the shadows are still banked up against the left-hand wall of the histogram the solution is to increase the amount of fill light, i.e. reduce the difference in brightness between the main light source and the fill light. If using flash as the source of your fill light it would be important to drop the power of the flash by at least two stops and choose the 'Slow-Sync' setting (a camera flash setting that balances both the ambient light exposure and flash exposure) so that the flash light does not overpower the main light source positioned behind your subject.

2. Before we massage the tones to create our low-key image we must first check that our tones are smooth and free from color and luminance noise. Zoom in to 100% magnification for an accurate preview and look for any problems in the smooth dark-toned areas. Setting both the Luminance Smoothing and Color Noise Reduction sliders to 25 (found in the Detail tab) removes the noise in this image. I would also recommend that the Sharpness slider be set to 0 at this point. Selective sharpening in the main editing space may help to keep the tones as smooth as possible rather than committing to global sharpening using the Adobe Camera RAW dialog box.

3. Create the low-key look by dropping the Exposure and/or the Brightness sliders in the Adjust tab. You can continue to drop these sliders until the highlights start to move away from the right-hand wall of the histogram. Select the 'White Balance tool' and move your mouse cursor over the deeper shadows - this will give you an idea of the RGB values you are likely to get when this image is opened into the editing space. Once you approach an average of 15 to 20 in all three channels the low-key look should have been achieved.

162

4. To enhance this image further a vignette has been added. This can be achieved in the Adobe Camera RAW dialog box in Photoshop CS2 but in Elements the vignette has to be added in the main editing space. In Elements 5.0 the new Correct Camera Distortion filter can be used to add the vignette. Just drag the Amount slider to the left to darken the corners. Dragging the Midpoint slider to the left will slowly move the darkening effect towards the centre of the image.

Note > If you are in 8 Bits/Channel mode and you want to add a vignette using layers, first create a new layer in Multiply mode and fill this layer with white. Hold down the Alt key as you click on the New Layer icon in the Layers palette to access the New Layer dialog box to give you these options.

5. To drop the RGB to Black and White I have used a technique that extracts the luminance values from the RGB file. I usually find that this gives a superior result to lowering the saturation or choosing the Remove Color command. Simply click the New Layer icon in the Layers palette and from the Fill Layer dialog box choose '50% Gray' as the contents color (Edit > Fill Layer > 50% Gray). Create a duplicate of the background layer (or merge the contents if you have placed the vignette on a separate layer) and then move this duplicate background layer to the top of the layers stack. Switch the mode of the background copy layer to 'Luminosity' to create a black and white image from the Luminance values. Choose 'Flatten Image' from the either the Layer palette's Fly-out menu or the Layer menu itself if the original Color values are no longer required.

6. To complete the project the file should be sharpened for printing. Photoshop Elements 5.0 now has an alternative to the Unsharp Mask. Adjust Sharpness (Enhance > Adjust Sharpness) is an excellent alternative for sharpening images that have little to no noise. To ensure the image does not appear over-sharpened be sure to restrict the radius to nothing higher than 1.5.

Note > If the Adjust Sharpness is making the smoother soft-focus tones appear anything but liquid smooth then consider a localized sharpening technique.

7. Duplicate the layer you wish to sharpen by dragging it to the New Layer icon in the Layers palette. Apply a generous amount of sharpening using either Unsharp Mask or Adjust Sharpness (be generous with the Amount slider but restrict the Radius slider to nothing greater than 1.5).

8. Click on the background layer, beneath the layer you have just sharpened, to make this the active layer. Then click on the Create Adjustment Layer icon in the Layers palette and choose a Levels adjustment layer from the pull-down menu. When the Levels dialog box opens make no adjustment – just click OK). Make sure this adjustment layer is below the duplicate layer. Click and drag it into position if it needs to move.

9. Fill the adjustment layer mask with black (Edit > Fill Layer > Black).

10. Click on the duplicate layer to make this the active layer. From the Layer menu choose 'Group with Previous'.

11. Select the Brush tool from the Tools palette. Select 'White' as the foreground color. Choose a soft brush from the Options bar and drop the opacity of the brush to 50%.

12. Click on the layer mask in the Layers palette to make this active and then move your attention to the main image window. Zoom the image to either 50% or Actual Pixels (100%). Paint in the areas where you would like to increase the sharpness of the image. Painting several times in the same region will slowly build up the sharpness of the image.

PERFORMANCE TIP - A FINAL WORD OF WARNING

To extract the maximum quality from your low-key image you will need to print this image on premium quality photo paper or have the image printed at a professional quality print service provider. All the work will be for nothing if the printer or surface quality of the paper cannot handle all of these smooth dark tones. If printed well the print will stand up to close - really close - scrutiny at close range.

part 3

montage

Project 1

Creative Montage

Masks are used to control which pixels are concealed or revealed on any image layer except the background layer. If the mask layer that has been used to conceal pixels is then discarded the original pixels reappear. This approach to montage work is termed 'non-destructive'. In the full version of Photoshop the mask is applied to the image layer whilst in Elements the mask is applied to a separate layer or the layer mask from an adjustment layer.

Forget cutting and pasting - learn the craft of professional montage using advanced masking techniques

1. Open the resource images and drag the layer thumbnail of the train driver image into the train's image window to create a file with two layers. Use the Move tool to position the second layer. Select 'Free Transform' to make minor changes in size of any new item being included in the montage.

2. Select the majority of the sky on Layer 1 by using a combination of the Magic Wand and Lasso tools. Keep the Shift key depressed to build on, or add to, each successive selection or use the 'Add to selection' and 'Subtract from selection' icons in the Options bar.

3. Use the Selection Brush tool in Mask mode to fine-tune the selection work. Pressing the Alt key when painting with the Selection Brush tool will remove rather than add to the selection or mask. Keep the feather set to 0 and the hardness of the Selection Brush tool set to maximum to match the quality of the Magic Wand. Switch the mode in the Options bar back to 'Selection' and from the Select menu choose 'Inverse'.

4. Select the background layer in the Layers palette and create a Levels adjustment layer. Select OK without making any adjustment. The selection has now become a mask that can be used to conceal the background pixels of the train driver. Click on Layer 1 at the top of the layers stack to select it and then choose 'Group with Previous' (Ctrl+G) from the Layer menu or hold down the Alt key as you move your mouse cursor over the dividing line between the train driver layer and the Levels adjustment layer and then click your mouse. The pixels are concealed rather than being deleted and can be retrieved if required to create the perfect edge.

PERFORMANCE TIP

This would be an ideal time to test drive the new Magic Selection Brush (a more sophisticated version of the Magic Wand tool). Start by painting on the background, even though Adobe encourages you to select the foreground (it is always quicker to select the area with fewer colors). An initial selection will then be made. Then proceed to add to your selection by clicking on the Indicate Foreground icon in the Options bar (even though you are selecting the background in this exercise) and then paint in any additional areas required for the selection.

If the selection invades any areas that you don't want, click on the Indicate Background icon and paint over these areas to perfect the selection. In this project the new tool does a fine job of working around the cigarette. Then choose 'Inverse' from the Select menu.

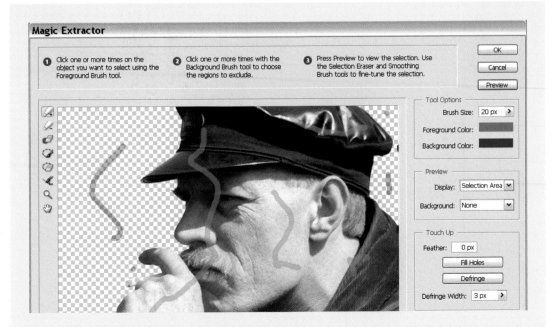

PERFORMANCE TIP

The fact of life is that some extractions can be as painful as pulling teeth! With this in mind Adobe offers you even more magic - the Magic Extractor (Image > Magic Extractor). This is yet another alternative for getting rid of problematic backgrounds. This tool takes a little more time than the Magic Selection Brush and is destructive in nature (it deletes the pixels you select with the Background Brush tool) so I would advise duplicating this layer before proceeding. As with the Magic Selection tool you make little marks or squiggles to advise Photoshop which pixels you would like to keep and which pixels you would like to delete. Then click on the Preview button. From the Preview menu choose a matte color to view your extracted subject (choose a different tone to the original background or one that is similar to the new background).

In the Touch Up section of the dialog box select a feather value (usually 1 or 2 pixels) and then choose a 'Defringe Width' to remove any of the remaining background. Not a bad job - if you don't mind losing the background pixels. If you do, then return to the main project to guide you through the basic techniques for professional, and 'non-automated', montage.

5. The mask will require some modifications before the edge is subtle and believable. Click on the layer mask thumbnail to select it. From the Filters menu select 'Blur > Gaussian Blur'. Select a pixel Radius that softens the edge of the subject by an appropriate amount (1 or 2 pixels is usually sufficient). If the subject has one edge that is softer than the rest, first make a selection to isolate that edge for individual attention. To remove the small halo or fringe pixels of the old background from around the subject go to the Filter menu and select 'Other > Maximum'. Select a pixel Radius amount that is just enough to shrink the mask so that the fringe of old background pixels disappears.

Note > Any small traces of old background (especially in corners or areas of fine detail) can be removed with the Brush tool. Paint at a reduced opacity (approximately 50%) and erase some of the mask in the localized area that is causing the problem.

PERFORMANCE TIP

Using Gaussian Blur and Minimum/Maximum filters to work the quality and position of an edge often leads to a visible edge to the layer. This should be removed by extending the mask in this area by either filling a selection or painting with black.

6. Select the background layer and create a Levels adjustment layer. Drag the Output Levels slider to a value of 200 to reduce the brightness of the distracting highlights in the background.

7. Select the train driver layer at the top of the Layers palette and then select 'Gradient Map' by clicking on the Create Adjustment Layer icon. Choose the "Blue/Copper" gradient preset that can be loaded from the supporting DVD or click on the gradient to edit an existing gradient map. See Part 2, Project 4: Toning (page 102) for more information on this technique.

8. Duplicate the background layer, and from the Filters menu choose 'Blur > Gaussian Blur'. Select a pixel Radius that reduces the focus sufficiently to separate the portrait from the background layer.

9. Create a Levels adjustment layer above the background layer and group the background copy with it as you did previously with the driver and the driver mask. Select the 'Gradient tool' with the 'Foreground (black) to Transparent' and 'Linear' options. Select the layer mask thumbnail and drag the Gradient tool in the main image window to follow the perspective line of the train. This gradient mask will conceal the front of the blurred train layer to create a simple depth of field effect.

Note > More elaborate 'depth masks' can be created using the selection tools. See Part 2, Project 1: Depth of Field (page 74).

10. Use the Clone Stamp set to 50% opacity to 'tone down' the distracting highlights on the background copy and/or background layer (top-left side of the image). This action makes way for the insertion of the wheels image in the top left-hand corner. Select the 'Circular Marquee tool' and draw a feathered circle around the wheel. With the active selection create a new adjustment layer.

11. Use the Type tool to create a line of text and click on the Create Warped Text icon in the Options bar and then select the 'Arc' option in the drop-down menu. Use a negative value to match the arc of the wheel. Select OK. The beauty of this montage technique is that any aspect is editable if the montage requires fine-tuning at a later date.

Project 2

Replacing a Sky

For people who seem to find themselves in the right place at the wrong time!
Have you ever traveled long and far to get to a scenic vista only to find that the
lighting is useless and the sky is a little short of inspiring? Do you make camp and
wait for the weather to change or reluctantly and humiliatingly buy the postcard?
Before you hit the Delete button or assign these 'almost rans' to a never-to-be-
opened-again folder to collect digital dust, consider the post-production alternatives.
Adobe lets you revisit these uninspired digital vistas to inject the mood that you were
looking for when you first whipped the camera from its case.

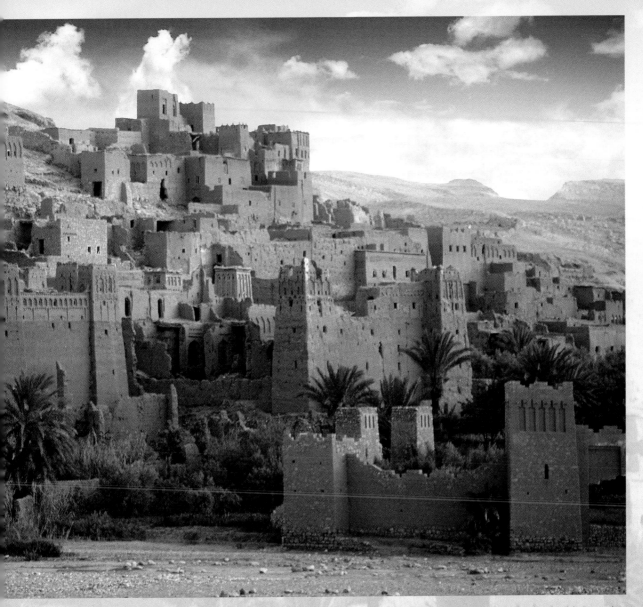

The Road to Morocco - change the sky to change the weather

I think every photographer can relate to the intrepid explorers of the Australian Outback who, after scaling the highest peak in the area with great expectations, decided to call it Mount Disappointment! One can only conclude that they were expecting to see something that was simply not there. This something extra could be made real so that all of your landscapes live up to your high expectations - with just a little digital help.

 Check out the supporting DVD to access an extensive stock library of royalty-free skies

This tutorial requires a little something you prepared earlier - a sky. It is worth making a little photographic collection of interesting skies for projects such as this one. A whole library of interesting skies can be found in the stock library on the supporting DVD.

1. Open the resource image and use the Magic Wand tool to select the sky. Select the Add to Selection icon in the Options bar to add additional areas of sky. Increasing the tolerance in the Options bar from the default setting will increase the amount of sky that is selected the first time.

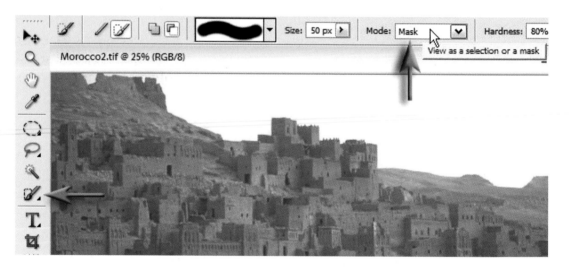

PERFORMANCE TIP

Clicking off the 'Contiguous' option in the Options bar will allow the Magic Wand tool to select areas of sky that may be surrounded by tree branches that would otherwise not have been selected without extensive clicking in Add to Selection mode. This may however cause highlights present in the image to be included in the selection. If this happens select the 'Lasso tool' with the 'Subtract from Selection' option and then encircle the areas you wish to remove from the overall selection. The Selection Brush tool can also be used to 'fine-tune' your selection. Select the 'Mask' option in the Options bar for a more accurate view of the selection area. Press the Alt or Option key to 'paint out' parts of the selection you do not require.

2. Zoom in on the edge that separates the sky from the rest of the landscape. You may find that the selection falls a little short. If this is the case go to 'Select > Modify > Expand' and then expand the selection by 1 or 2 pixels. Click OK and then zoom in on the edge of the selection to see if this improves the positioning of the selection.

3. To prevent the new sky looking as though it has been cut out of a magazine and stuck onto your image it is important to create a 'feathered' edge for the selection (something that will create a soft and seamless transition). Go to 'Select > Feather' and enter a 1- or 2-pixel Feather Radius. When the mask is accurate switch back to the 'Selection' option in the Options bar.

4. It is advisable to save any important selections that you have made to prevent your selection being accidentally lost. Go to 'Select > Save Selection' and name your selection with an original name such as 'Sky'. After saving a selection you will be able to impress your friends by loading a selection with the words 'here is something I prepared earlier'. Save the changes to the edited file so the selection can be loaded even after the image has been closed and then reopened.

5. Open the image with the sky you wish to import. Click and drag the sky thumbnail in the Layers palette into the Morocco image window. The sky should have similar pixel dimensions to that of the host image. If the images do not precisely match you can, however, use the Transform > Free Transform command to resize your sky to fit.

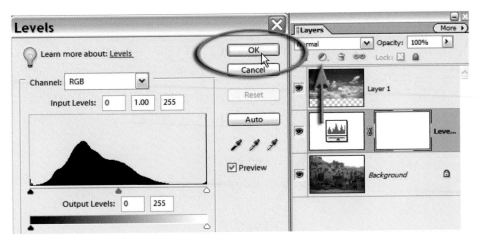

6. Click on the background layer in the Layers palette to make it the active layer and then add a Levels adjustment layer. Select OK without making any adjustment (we only need the layer mask and not the adjustment itself).

7. To restrict or limit the visibility of the new sky to the correct area we need to load the selection that we saved earlier. Go to the Select menu and choose 'Load Selection'. Choose your named selection, check the 'Invert' option and click OK. With your active selection and the layer mask of the Levels adjustment layer selected choose the 'Fill Selection' option from the Edit menu and choose 'Black' from the Contents menu. The final step in the process is to select the sky layer and from the Layer menu choose 'Group with Previous'.

8. Select the 'Move tool' and choose the best position for the new sky by dragging it in the main image window. It is not going to look perfect just yet as most skies get progressively lighter as they near the horizon. If the sky you are importing does not have this quality it can easily be fixed in a two-step process.

9. Hold down the Alt key and create another Levels adjustment layer. The Layers dialog box that opens gives you the option to 'Group' this adjustment layer with the previous layer. This will restrict the adjustments we are about to make to only the sky component of the image. Click OK and when the Levels dialog box opens make the entire sky much lighter by dragging the Gamma slider most of the way to the left. Select OK to close the Levels dialog box.

To fade or lighten the sky progressively towards the top of the hills start by selecting the default 'Foreground' and 'Background' colors in the Tools palette. You may need to switch the colors to ensure black is the foreground color. Select the 'Gradient tool' with the 'Foreground to Background, and 'Linear Gradient' options from the Options bar. Drag a gradient from the top of the frame to just above the top of the hills. If the effect is anything other than 'cool', hit the 'Edit > Undo', check the settings and try again.

10. Zoom in to 100% Actual pixels or 200% and use the spacebar to drag the image along the seam between the host image and its new sky. If you detect any white halos or loss of fine detail along this edge we can adjust the position of the edge to create a perfect match. Select the 'layer mask' at the base of the clipping group and from the Enhance > Adjust Lighting menu select 'Levels'. Moving the Gamma slider either to the left or to the right should perfect the visual appearance.

Note > More adjustment can be provided by using either the Maximum or Minimum filters from the Filter > Other menu.

PERFORMANCE TIP

If an initial adjustment to the layer mask fixes the majority of the edge accuracy, but leaves an inaccurate section, you should proceed to make a feathered selection of the offending area (use the Lasso tool or a Marquee tool with a 3- to 5-pixel Feather Radius), then reapply a Levels adjustment. The resulting modification will be restricted to the selected area only.

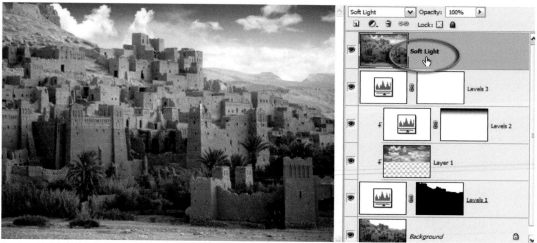

11. When replacing a sky you can aim to match the light quality found in the host image with that likely to be provided by the new, but more interesting, sky. There are examples of skies on the supporting DVD that would provide soft, filtered, sunny, warm or cool lighting to any scene. If however the new sky looks altogether more sunny than the one you have replaced, you may need to warm up the scene you are working on and increase the contrast to suit.

In this image the entire image is made warmer and brighter using a Levels adjustment layer. Adjust the individual channels to increase the red component and reduce the blue component. A neat trick to add some warmth and contrast is to stamp the visible elements to a new layer (Ctrl+Alt+Shift and then type E) and set the blend mode to 'Soft Light'.

Now that you have spread a little sunshine around you may like to consider the words of an old pop song 'Everywhere you go, always take the weather with you'. With Adobe rendering the world with an altogether sunnier outlook, alternative realities are always a possibility. May your landscapes always bask in beautiful/interesting weather!

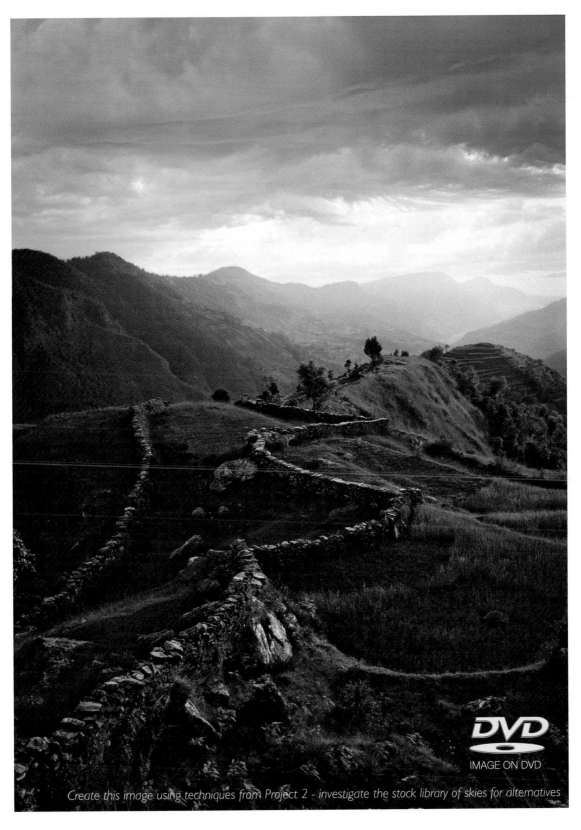

IMAGE ON DVD

Create this image using techniques from Project 2 - investigate the stock library of skies for alternatives

Project 3

RAW IMAGES ON DVD

High Dynamic Range

Contrary to popular opinion, what you see is not always what you get. You may be able to see the detail in those dark shadows and bright highlights when the sun is shining - but can your image sensor? Contrast in a scene is often a photographer's worst enemy. Contrast is a sneak thief that steals away the detail in the highlights or shadows (sometimes both).

Contrast no problem - discover the secrets to limitless dynamic range

Wedding photographers will deal with the problem of contrast by using fill-flash to lower the subject contrast; commercial photographers diffuse their own light source or use additional fill lighting and check for missing detail using the Histogram or a Polaroid. Landscape photographers however have drawn the short straw when it comes to solving the contrast problem. For the landscape photographer there is no 'quick fix'. A reflector that can fill the shadows of the Grand Canyon has yet to be made and diffusing the sun's light is only going to happen if the clouds are prepared to play ball.

Method 1 - using a single camera RAW file

The first technique the photographer can use to combat extreme subject contrast utilizes the flexibility of the Camera RAW format (an image format that can be selected in most high-end digicams and all DSLR cameras). If you are able to capture in RAW mode you will be able to exploit the full dynamic range that your image sensor is capable of. Choosing the JPEG format in your camera when photographing high contrast subjects may result in the loss of shadow and highlight detail (see Part 1, Project 3: Camera RAW, page 22). Part 2 of this project offers an option for merging two separate exposures to restore highlight and shadow detail.

When the RAW file is opened in Photoshop Elements the Exposure slider in the camera RAW dialog box allows the user to choose an increased or decreased exposure setting from the one that was selected in-camera and used to capture the image. This allows the photographer to access either increased highlight information or increased shadow information after the image has been captured. It is possible to open multiple versions of the same RAW file in the Photoshop Elements' editing space if you save each version using a different name.

Note > When the RAW information is processed the preview and thumbnail of the RAW file reflects these preferences but the RAW data cannot itself be modified. This RAW file can be processed a second time with a different set of preferences for exposure, color and tone.

To achieve the optimum dynamic range that is possible from the information recorded by the image sensor (increased shadow detail AND increased highlight detail) we can open two images from the same RAW file, each file being optimized for a different end of the exposure range. In Photoshop Elements we can then simply merge the two exposures together. Some would call this manipulation when in reality all we are doing is restoring the tonality back to how our human vision first saw the scene rather than how the camera interpreted it.

1. Open your camera RAW file in the Adobe camera RAW dialog box. Move the Exposure slider to the right until the shadow detail has opened up and the detail is clearly visible. Pay no attention to the highlights that will now be overexposed. If you have the Shadows and Highlights boxes checked, the color red indicates that massive amounts of highlight detail are being lost or 'clipped'. Notice however how the tall peaks on the left-hand side of the histogram move away from the left side as you move the Exposure slider to the right. If the shadows are rich in detail but appear flat and gray you can compensate for these by raising both the Contrast and Saturation sliders. Zoom in to 100% and check the shadows for excessive noise. If noise is a problem proceed to the Detail tab and raise the Luminance Smoothing and Color Noise Reduction sliders to the right until the noise is sufficiently suppressed. Set the 'Depth' in the lower left-hand corner of the dialog box to 8 Bits/Channel and select 'Open'.

2. The image will now open in the main editing space and the camera RAW dialog box will close with your settings saved. Go to the File menu and choose 'Save As'. Give your file a name like RAW_blend1 or RAW_shadows. It is important to save and rename the RAW file that has been opened into the main editing space first before proceeding, otherwise things can get confusing when your try to open the file again.

3. When the RAW file opens in the RAW dialog box for the second time you can now move the Exposure slider to the left to optimize the image for the highlight detail. Choose an appropriate setting for the Contrast and Saturation sliders and again select the Open button.

Note > In the example some highlight clipping remains even with an exposure setting of –1.75. If you are presented with this scenario the only way of achieving additional information is to bracket the exposures whilst the camera is mounted securely on a tripod during the initial capture.

4. Now that you have created two images from the camera RAW file you can start to combine the best features of each exposure. There is no need to save and rename the second darker image. Click anywhere on the darker image to make it active. Now go to the Layers palette and click on the thumbnail image and drag it to the image window of the other image (the one you have saved and renamed). Hold down the Shift key as you let go of the thumbnail to ensure that both exposures are perfectly aligned.

5. The next step involves adding a layer mask that will be used to conceal the darker features of the top layer. To create an adjustment layer for this purpose first select the background layer in the Layers palette and then click on the Create Adjustment Layer icon and choose 'Levels'. Do not make any adjustment in this dialog box but simply select OK.

6. You will now 'Group' the top layer with this adjustment layer to link the layer mask to this image layer. Click on the top layer to make this the active layer and then from the Layer menu choose 'Group with Previous'.

7. In the Tools palette choose the 'Gradient tool' and from the Options bar choose the 'Black, White' gradient, 'Linear' option with an Opacity of 100%. Click on the layer mask to make this the active component of the layer.

PERFORMANCE TIP

A more complex mask is often called for when the subject is not so clearly defined as a bright sky and a dark foreground. If this is the case you can paint directly into the mask using a soft-edged brush with the foreground color set to 'Black' and the opacity dropped to 50%.

8. Move the cursor into the image window and click just below the horizon line. Hold down the Shift key and drag the gradient to a position just above the sun and then let go of the mouse clicker. This action will add a gradient to the layer mask and will act to hide the darker foreground pixels in the top layer. We will now be able to view the sky from the image with the decreased exposure and the foreground from the image with the increased exposure.

9. To create the right balance between the foreground and background it may be necessary to fine-tune the image. We could have increased the contrast and saturation of the decreased exposure in the RAW dialog box but it was difficult to gain an idea of what the two images would look like when combined at this stage of the process. In this project it was decided to duplicate the top layer (drag the layer to the New Layer icon in the Layers palette) and then switch the mode to 'Overlay'. You will notice that the duplicated layer is still part of the group and so the mask shields this layer as well as the layer beneath. The 'Overlay' blend mode has the effect of increasing both the contrast and the saturation of the sky. The effect is that the image now looks like how I remembered the scene when I first raised the camera to my eye.

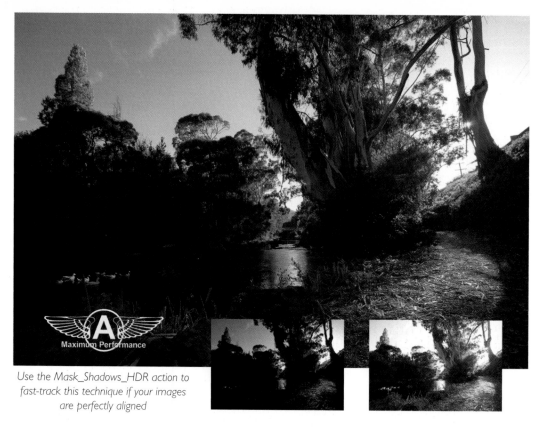

Use the Mask_Shadows_HDR action to fast-track this technique if your images are perfectly aligned

Method 2 - bracketing exposures

1. If we can't fit all the goodies in one exposure, then we'll just have to take two or more. The idea is to montage, or blend, the best of both worlds (the light and dark side of the camera's, not quite, all seeing eye). To make the post-production easier we need to take a little care in the pre-production, i.e. mount the camera securely on a sturdy tripod. Take two exposures - one overexposing from the auto reading, and the other underexposing from the auto reading. One or two stops either side of the meter-indicated exposure should cover most high-contrast situations.

PERFORMANCE TIP

Setting your camera to 'auto bracket exposure mode' means that you don't have to touch the camera between the two exposures, thereby ensuring the first and second exposures can be exactly aligned with the minimum of fuss. Unfortunately for me, the little Fuji FinePix s7000 I was using for this image has auto bracket exposure but it is not operational in RAW capture mode - the only respectable format for self-respecting landscape photographers. This is where you dig out your trusty cable release and, if you are really lucky, have somewhere to screw it into! The only other movement to be aware of is something beyond your control. If there is a gale blowing (or even a moderate gust) you are not going to get the leaves on the trees to align perfectly in post-production. This also goes for fast-moving clouds and anything else that is likely to be zooming around in the fraction of a second between the first and second exposures.

2. Select the 'Move tool' in the Tools palette and drag the dark underexposed image into the window of the lighter overexposed image (alternatively just drag the thumbnail from the Layers palette with any tool selected). Holding down the Shift key as you let go of the image will align the two layers (but not necessarily the two images).

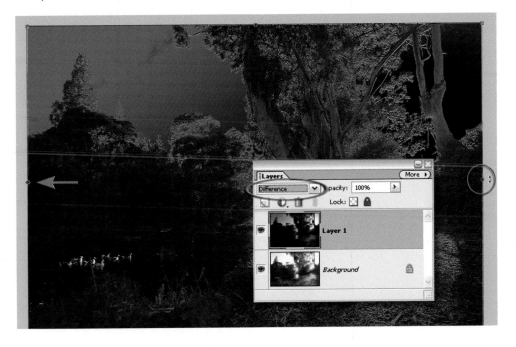

3. In the Layers palette set the blend mode of the top layer to 'Difference' to check the alignment of the two images. If they align no white edges will be apparent (usually the case if the tripod was sturdy and the two exposures were made via an auto feature or cable release). If you had to resort to a friend's right shoulder you will now spend the time you thought you had saved earlier. To make a perfect alignment you need to select 'Free Transform' from the Image > Transform menu. Nudge the left side into alignment and then move the reference point location in the Options bar to the left-hand side of the square. Highlight the numbers in the rotation field in the Options bar and then rotate the image into final alignment.

4. Add a Levels adjustment layer above the background layer. Make no adjustments as only the mask is required. Group the top layer with this adjustment layer (hold down the Alt key as you click on the dividing line between the two layers). Click on the background layer and choose 'All' from the Select menu (Ctrl+A). Copy to the clipboard and then Alt+Click the adjustment layer thumbnail. The image window should appear white as the layer mask is empty. Now choose 'Paste' from the edit menu (Ctrl+V). Apply a small amount of Gaussian Blur to this mask before Alt+Clicking once again to return to the normal view.

5. It is important to recreate the expanded contrast of the original scene otherwise the image will look slightly surreal if the overall contrast is low. The first technique to expand the contrast is to apply a Levels adjustment to this layer mask (Ctrl+L). Drag in the Output sliders (directly beneath the Shadow and Highlight sliders) until the final contrast appears high but not clipped (lowering the contrast of the mask increases the contrast of the final image).

6. The observant amongst us will have noticed the ducks have been breeding. The ghost images can be removed by painting or cloning them out on both the top layer and the layer mask beneath. If using a soft edged brush to paint them out you should first sample an adjacent color by holding down the Alt key and clicking on the surrounding tone. Alt+click the layer mask to get a clear idea of what you are doing.

7. In order to achieve the final contrast setting for this image, stamp the visible elements to a new layer (Ctrl+Alt+Shift then type the letter E) and place this new layer in Overlay or Soft Light mode. Adjust the opacity of this layer until the required effect is created. If the shadow tones are rendered too dark by this process a Levels adjustment layer can be grouped with this layer and the Shadows Output slider raised to restrict the increase in contrast to just the midtones and highlight tones.

PERFORMANCE TIP

In the full version of Photoshop the user has access to the 'Advanced Blending Options'. In this dialog box it is possible to reduce the opacity of the shadow tones on the top layer to reveal the shadow tones beneath. The effect can be faded in gradually creating a blend of the optimum highlights from the top layer and the optimum shadow tones of the background layer. The advanced blending options are only available to users of the full version of Photoshop, but the same results can be achieved using a layer style preset loaded into the presets folder in Elements. The layer styles provided on the support DVD give the Elements user the option of partial transparency based on tonality.

Photoshop Elements users can access the Transparency Layer style by first loading the preset that is available on the supporting DVD into the Layer Styles folder (C: Drive > Documents and Settings > All Users > Application Data > Adobe > Photoshop Elements > 5.0 > Photo Creations > Special Effects > Layer Styles). The preset was created in the full version of Photoshop but can be read by Photoshop Elements. The software must be restarted after loading the preset into the folder before Elements can find it.

Select the top layer in the Layers palette and then click on each of the four presets in turn (now located in the Styles and Effects palette) and choose the one that renders the best tonality.

Create an adjustment layer by clicking on the Create New Adjustment Layer icon and choose 'Levels' from the menu. The final step in the process is to target the deepest shadows and brightest highlights to the values best suited to your chosen output device. My own Epson inkjet paper handles the highlights really well and tones of 250 are easily distinguishable from the paper white (255). The precise targeting of the shadow tones is dependent on the inks and paper being used and can be anywhere between 10 and 20. Do not rely on your monitor at this stage if your final output is print - if in doubt print a test strip and readjust the target points if required. To target a tone refer to Project 4 in Part 1. Select OK when you are satisfied your image is looking fabulous.

Note > Finding the optimum values for your printer and media can be achieved by printing a tonal step wedge with known values to plot what your printer is capable of.

Project 4

Creative Type

Elements may be a couple of tools short of a six-pack when it comes to working with vector shapes and paths, the principal tools of the trade for graphic designers, but creative typography is one area where Elements users do not have to bow down their heads in shame. We can be subtle and sophisticated, using conservative and delicate fonts with carefully color-matched hues or, for those of you who believe typography does not always have to whisper, here are a couple of major techniques we can employ to get our message across loud and clear.

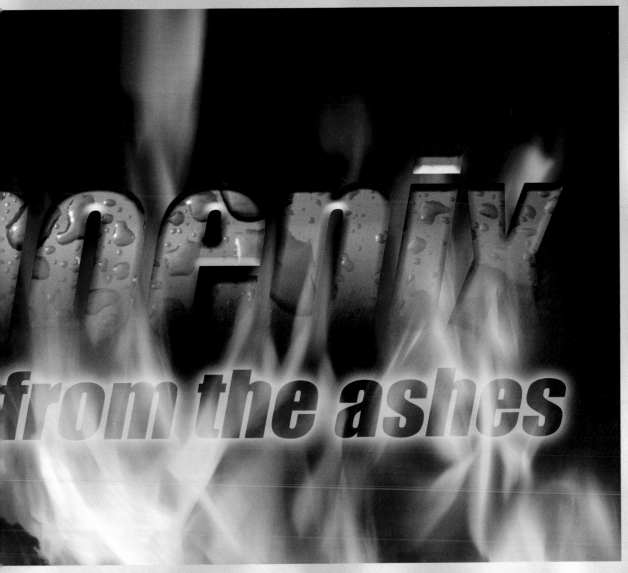

phoenix

from the ashes

Master the techniques for working creatively with text layers and images to create stunning graphics

1. Open the Fire image from the supporting DVD. Select the 'Type tool' in the Tools palette and then specify the font, style and size of the text.

Note > Color is normally selected by clicking the color swatch. Color is not important for this exercise as the type will be filled with another image. Ensure that anti-aliased option is selected (highlighted) to ensure smooth edged type and then click OK.

2. Stretch or distort the type layer by applying the Free Transform command (Ctrl+T). The type in the example is stretched vertically by dragging the top-center handle upwards. Press the Enter key to apply the transformation.

PERFORMANCE TIP

'Transform' alters the shape and/or size of the subject matter on a single selected layer. Holding the Shift key down whilst dragging a corner handle will constrain the proportions. Holding down the Ctrl key whilst dragging a handle will allow you to skew the text.

3. Apply an effect or layer style to this text layer. Choose 'Bevels > Simple Inner' from the Style flyout menu in the Options bar.

PERFORMANCE TIP

The appearance of the bevel can be fine-tuned by going to 'Layer > Layer Style > Style Settings'. The Style Settings dialog box can also be accessed by double-clicking on the Layer Style icon on the layer in the Layers palette.

4. Open the image containing the texture you wish to paste into the text. For maximum quality check that the pixel dimensions of the texture image are the same or greater than the image containing the text. The size can be modified later using the Free Transform command but the digital photographer must be careful not to increase the size of any image excessively ('interpolation' has a tendency to lower the overall quality). Drag the thumbnail of the drops in the Layers palette into the image window containing the fire and text. The texture will be placed on a layer above the other layers completely concealing both the text and the background.

5. A clipping group is required in order to fill the text with the image of the raindrops. Go to 'Layer > Group with Previous' or move the mouse cursor to the line that divides the two layers in the Layers palette. By holding down the Alt key the Clipping icon should appear (two overlapping circles). Clicking whilst holding down the Alt key will group the layers together. The layer thumbnail is indented, the name of the base layer in the group is underlined, and the text acts as a mask.

6. Switch off the visibility of the background layer by clicking on the eye in the Layers palette. Stamp the visible elements to a new layer (hold down the Ctrl, Alt and Shift keys whilst typing the letter E on the keyboard). The text will appear on its own layer filled with raindrops. You can now switch on the visibility of the background layer. The visibility of the text layer directly above the background layer can now be switched off as it has served its purpose.

7. Select 'Layer 1' in the Layers palette (the raindrops layer) and then create a Levels adjustment layer. As we only require the adjustment layer mask we can simply click OK without making any adjustments. Group 'Layer 2' with this Levels adjustment layer.

Note > When the Phoenix layer is grouped with the adjustment layer no visible change occurs at this stage as the adjustment layer mask is empty.

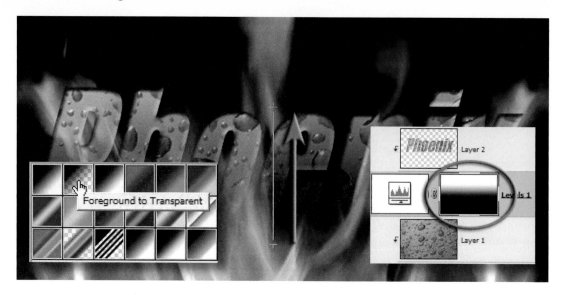

8. Set the default foreground and background colors in the Tools palette and then type the letter X on the keyboard to switch the colors to black in the foreground and white in the background. Select the 'Gradient tool' in the Tools palette. Select the 'Linear gradient', 'Foreground to Background' or 'Black, White' options and 100% opacity. Move the cursor to the bottom of the typography in the main image window. Click and drag the gradient cursor from the base of the letters to the top of the letters. A linear gradient will appear in the layer mask and the typography should be half hidden behind this layer mask. Experiment with dragging shorter and longer gradients.

9. The layer mask can be moved by selecting the 'Move tool' and dragging inside the main image window. To move the text instead of the mask you must first click on the layer above the adjustment layer. To move the layer mask and the typography at the same time you must first link the layers. Hold down the Shift key and click on both of the layers in the group to select them, then click on the Link Layers icon in the Layers palette. The mask and the text can now be moved together.

PERFORMANCE TIP

To adjust the color of the text (now that it is not controlled by the font color) you can add an adjustment layer to the existing group. Hold down the Alt key as you select an adjustment layer to open the New Layer options dialog box. Select the Group With Previous Layer box to ensure the adjustment affects only the text and not the background layer.

10. Select the 'Horizontal Type tool' again and click beneath the word you have just created. Select a smaller point size and type the words 'rises from the ashes'. Adjust the size and position of the text so that it is exactly the same width as the word 'Phoenix' (see step 2) .

Note > Holding down the Shift key as you click with the text cursor ensures you always create a new text layer rather than editing the existing text layer. This is not a problem in this step as the visibility of the original text layer is off.

11. Apply a Simple Glow from the Outer Glow layer styles to this text layer. Return to the Style menu and select 'Hide' from the Visibility menu. This action hides the text color but leaves the layer style at 100% opacity. Adjust the Outer Glow size using the Style Settings palette (see the performance tip in step 3).

PERFORMANCE TIP - AN ALTERNATIVE APPROACH

An alternative approach to masking the text and texture is possible. The advantage of this approach is that the text remains editable as the text is not rasterized (converted from a text layer into a pixel layer). The disadvantage of this approach is that a more sophisticated mask is required to mask both the texture and the text, and this can take a little longer to perfect.

The text and texture are grouped with the adjustment layer mask containing the linear gradient.

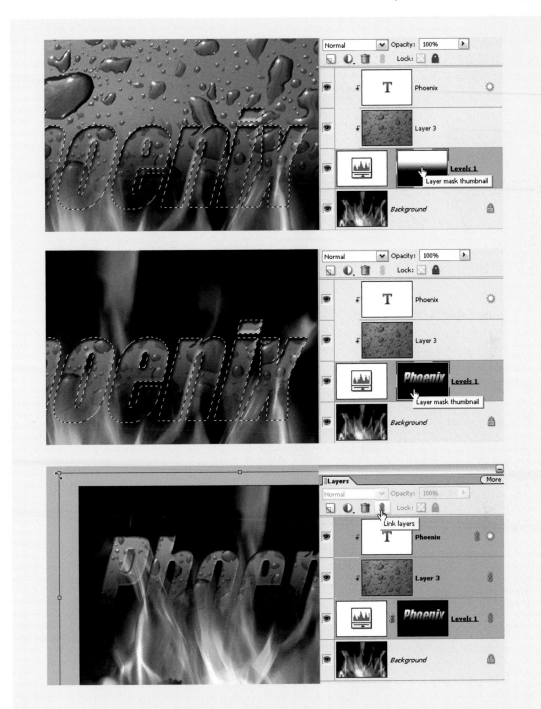

Ctrl+Click the text layer to load the outline of the text as a selection. Invert the selection (Shift+Ctrl+I) and then select the layer mask thumbnail and fill the selection with black (Alt+ Backspace if black is the foreground color). Use the Maximum or Minimum filters, if required, to perfect the mask.

PERFORMANCE TIP

Creative text styles can be accessed via the Artwork and Effects palette. Text styles can be found in both the Add Text category and Layer Styles in Special Effects. Filters can also be applied but this requires the user to 'Simplify' the layer (convert the text to pixels), which will prevent you from editing the text later on.

When applying a layer style to your text layer be sure to double-click the Layer Styles icon on the layer to open the Style Settings dialog box. These styles can be dramatically altered by changing the settings or switching off component aspects of the layer style.

The styles available in your Photoshop Elements software are just the tip of the iceberg when it comes to creative possibilities. If you want your type to look like wood, metal, plastic, rock or even tree bark then there is a free style waiting for you online at Adobe Studio Exchange.

HTTP://SHARE.STUDIO.ADOBE.COM

Above are just a few examples of the possibilities that layer styles can afford the creative individual. A Maximum Performance Text Styles folder is available on the DVD that accompanies this book. Just place the folder in the Styles folder in the Presets folder and use the same procedure outlined in the previous project and the introductory section of the book to load the styles into your Special Effects library. The last two examples were downloaded from the Adobe Studio Exchange website and are from the Australian Bush series by BSeen and the Stonemason series by CSP. More than a thousand others are available at http://share.studio.adobe.com.

Project 5

JAGUAR

Displacement

Create a showpiece montage by elevating an old Jag into a classic motor with a little spit and polish and some delectable digital deeds. Wickedly good stuff! The car's paintwork was enhanced before starting the project by increasing the overall saturation of the image and the scratches were removed using the Healing Brush. The tires were made to look like new by using the Burn tool set to 20%. If only it was this easy in real life!

Liquid pixels - a displacement, masking and layer style 'combo'

Stage 1 - Creating a backdrop using the Displacement filter

The layer blend modes are an effective way of merging or blending a pattern or graphic with a three-dimensional form. By using the blend modes the flag in this project can be modified to respect the color and tonality of the undulating silk beneath it. The highlights and shadows that give the silk its shape can however be further utilized to wrap or bend the flag so that it obeys the material's shape and sense of volume. This can be achieved by using the Displace filter in conjunction with a 'displacement map'. The 'map' defines the contours to which the flag must conform. The final effect can be likened to 'shrink-wrapping' the flag to the 3-D form of the undulating silk.

How it works: The brightness level of each pixel in the map directs the filter to shift the corresponding pixel of the selected layer in a horizontal or vertical plane. The principle on which this technique works is that of 'mountains and valleys'. Dark pixels in the map shift the graphic pixels down into the shaded valleys of the 3-D form whilst the light pixels of the map raise the graphic pixels onto the illuminated peaks of the 3-D form.

1. A silk dressing gown was photographed using the available light. For this image to act as an effective displacement map the contrast must however be expanded. An effective way of expanding contrast in Photoshop Elements is to duplicate the layer and set the top layer to 'Overlay' blend mode. Note the changes to the histogram by viewing the histogram in the Histogram palette.

Note > Duplicate the silk image resource file to ensure the original file is retained as a master and not lost by this manipulation. Either copy the image file before you start the project or go to 'File > Duplicate' before you proceed to step 2.

2. Go to the Image menu and from the Mode submenu select 'Grayscale'. Choose the option 'Flatten' when the Warning dialog box appears.

Note > The displacement map must be in Grayscale otherwise the color channels will upset the appropriate displacement effect.

3. To further improve the effectiveness of the displacement map we must blur the image slightly. This effect of blurring the map will smooth out the lines of the flag as it wraps around the contours of the silk. Too much blur and the undulations will be lost, too little and the lines of the flag will appear jagged as it is upset by any minor differences in tone. Go to 'Filter > Blur > Gaussian Blur' and start by selecting a Radius of around 10 pixels. Increase or decrease this radius when working with images of a different resolution.

4. Save the image (displacement map) as a Photoshop (PSD) file. Close the blurred Grayscale file as the map is now complete. You will need to choose this file when the Displacement filter asks for the location of your map, so make a note of where it has been saved to on your computer.

5. Open or select the RGB silk file that has not been blurred. Also open the flag image. With the flag image as the active window, choose 'All' from the Select menu and then choose 'Copy' from the File menu. Now make the silk image the active window and choose 'Paste' from the File menu. Alternatively you can just drag the thumbnail of the flag image in the Layers palette into the image window of the silk image if you can see both image windows on your desktop.

Set the blend mode of the flag layer to 'Multiply'. If you are intending to displace a graphic or a texture it is worth ensuring that you have some elbow room (when we displace the flag it will come away from, and reveal, the edges of the background layer if they are the same size). Use the Free Transform command to enlarge the flag layer so that it is a little larger than the background layer.

6. Go to 'Filter > Distort > Displace'. Enter in the amount of displacement in the Horizontal and Vertical fields of the Displace dialog box. The size of the displacement is dependent on the resolution of the image you are working on. Choose amounts of 40 for both fields for the Flag.jpg used in this project. Increasing the amount greater than 60 for either the Horizontal or Vertical scale will increase the amount of distortion in this project image, but will also start to break off islands of color from the design of the flag indicating that the limit of the effect has been exceeded. Choose the displacement map you created earlier to complete this step. Your flag should now miraculously conform to the contours of the silk. If you are not entirely happy with the results go to the Edit menu and choose 'Undo'. Repeat the process choosing smaller or greater amounts in the Displace dialog box.

Note > It helps if the graphic or pattern image file you are displacing is slightly larger than the image file you created the map for. This will ensure that no gaps appear between the distorted graphic and the edge of the image window.

7. Add an adjustment layer and drag the Highlight slider to the start of the histogram to extend the dynamic range and make the highlights and midtones appear brighter. Your dramatic and colorful background is now complete.

Stage 2 - Creating a montage using masks

The following montage techniques are used for professional results. The techniques covered allow precise control over the alignment and quality of the edge (soft/hard) to ensure that no halos from the old background are visible (even when using crude selection tools such as the Magic Wand).

Note > Download the completed flag file from the supporting DVD if you would like to start the project at this point.

8. Open the image of the Jaguar car and add this as a layer above the adjustment layer and flag in the master project file (see step 5 for a guide on combining two images). I have made the background behind the car white in order to make it easier for you to remove it from view in this project. You can use one of two different methods in order to hide the white background from view.

Method 1 > Select the 'Magic Wand tool' in the Tools palette. Select the Add To icon in the Options bar and set the tolerance in the Options bar to 20. Click on the white background surrounding the car and then click on the rear window behind the back seat to add these sections to the selection. You do not need to delete the white background in order to conceal it (deleting pixels is considered destructive editing and can restrict the control over the edge quality later).

Note > The TIFF image on the supporting DVD has a saved selection of the car.

CUSTOM SHAPES ON DVD

Method 2 > Elements 5.0 does not have a Pen tool for the creation of paths but you can use them in the form of Custom Shapes if they are available to load into the Shapes folder. I have saved a custom shape for both the car and the leaping Jaguar used in the final montage. Locate the Application folder for Photoshop Elements 5.0 and then drag the shapes files for this project into the Custom Shapes folder (located in the Presets folder). Restart Elements, click on the Cookie Cutter tool in the Tools palette, choose XJ6 from the Cookie menu and from the 'Shape' options choose 'Defined Size' and a 1-pixel feather. Click in the image window and drag the cookie shape over the car until it aligns. Let go of the mouse clicker to see the results of the cutting action and perfect the cutting action by nudging the shape into alignment using the arrow keys on the keyboard. Commit the Cutting action by clicking on the tick in the Options bar. To proceed to the next step you will need to load the car as a selection. Hold down the Ctrl key and click on the layer. A selection of the car will appear.

Note > The Cookie Cutter technique deletes rather than hides the white background pixels, but as the cookie cutter outline is smoother and more accurate than can probably be achieved using the selection tools, the warning about deleting rather than hiding pixels in Method 1 can largely be ignored.

9. If you selected the background using the Magic Wand tool then you will need to go to the Select menu and choose 'Inverse Selection'. If you have used the Cookie Cutter technique hold the Ctrl key down and click on the layer thumbnail to load the car as a selection. Then proceed to select an adjustment layer from the Layers palette. It does not matter which adjustment layer you choose as we will only be borrowing its layer mask and not using it to make any adjustments to the layers beneath. Just select OK without making any adjustment. Click on the car layer above the adjustment layer and choose 'Group' from the Layer menu.

Note > The background has already been removed using the cookie cutter but the edge still requires masking to improve its appearance.

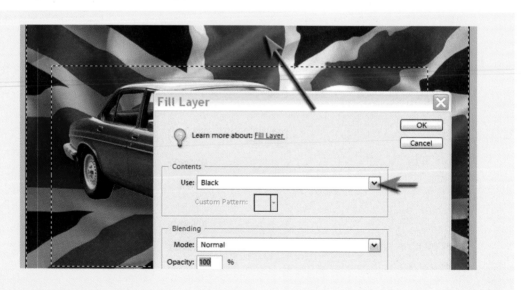

PERFORMANCE TIP

The resulting mask is likely to have a 1-pixel white line visible around the edge of the old background. To remove this thin white line paint with black directly into the layer mask of the adjustment layer. Alternatively a quicker option (if you know your shortcuts) is to make a rectangular selection around the car using the Marquee tool (M), invert the selection (Ctrl+Shift+I) and fill this selection with black (Alt+Backspace if black is in the foreground swatch).

10. Zoom in to 100 or 200% and take a good close look at the edge. The edge needs to be softened and moved to conceal the remnants of the old white background. From the Filter menu choose 'Blur > Gaussian Blur'. Use a Radius value of 1 or 2 pixels to soften the edge of the outline of the car (if you used the Cookie Cutter tool the outline will already have been softened by 1 pixel). Larger values are required in montage work when dealing with very high-resolution images or masking objects that were not photographed in sharp focus.

11. Go to 'Filter > Other > Minimum' and choose a 1- or 2-pixel Radius to eliminate the remnants of the white background. The filter acts to expand the mask and limit the visibility of the pixels on the layer above.

PERFORMANCE TIP

The mask can be fine-tuned by applying a Levels adjustment to this layer mask (yes - you really can apply a Levels adjustment to a Levels adjustment layer mask). Moving the central Gamma slider in the Levels dialog box moves the edge of the mask if it has been first softened as in step 10. Levels offers a little more control that the Maximum and Minimum filters in that you can also move the Shadow and Highlight sliders to control both the trailing edge and leading edge independently. Pretty cool stuff!

12. Select the layer below the mask layer and then click on the New Layer icon in the Layers palette. Select the 'Selection Brush tool' in the Tools palette and then paint a selection that extends just in front of the tires and underneath the car. Extend some way over the edge of the car as this will be needed later (blurring the shadow will reduce its opacity at the edges). From the Edit menu choose the Fill command and select 'Black' as the color and click OK.

13. Apply a Gaussian Blur filter to this layer and then refine the shadow by setting the blend mode to 'Multiply' and lowering the opacity to around 70%.

Note > A second shadow layer could be added to create some smaller shadows just underneath the wheels and further underneath the car. This refinement will help create the illusion that the car is in contact with the flag.

14. The image just needs a few finishing touches to complete the project. Add the leaping Jaguar. This time delete the white background pixels instead of masking them. A custom shape and saved selection are available for this leaping Jaguar on the supporting DVD. Ctrl+Click the layer to load the Jaguar as a selection. Create a new layer underneath the leaping Jaguar and fill the selection with black (Edit > Fill Selection). Group these two layers (Layer > Group with Previous). The base layer now acts as a mask and should be modified by applying the Gaussian Blur filter (to soften the edge) and Maximum filter (Filter > Other > Maximum) to remove any white fringe pixels.

15. As the Jaguar does not need to appear to be in contact with the flag we can simply add a drop shadow to this layer rather than create a shadow by hand. Click on a Drop Shadow style in the Styles palette. This can be modified or perfected by going to the Layers menu and choosing 'Style Settings'. The angle and distance of the shadow from the object can be controlled from this dialog box or the user can simply click inside the image window and drag the shadow to a different position to obtain the best effect.

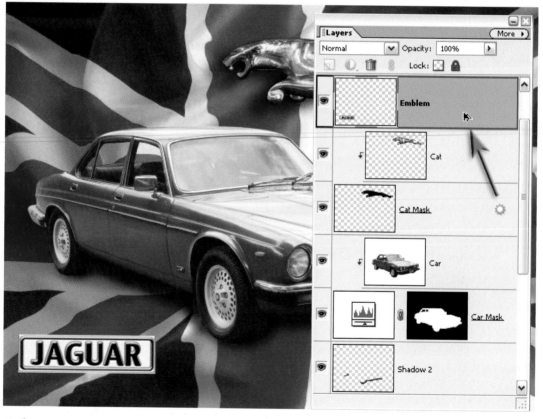

16. Complete the image by adding the image of the badge in the lower left-hand corner. Add a drop shadow to this layer and the project is complete. Download the American flag to turn a home-grown tired old car from yesteryear into a classic motor fit for the photo frame.

TIFF WITH SAVED
SELECTION ON DVD

car photograph courtesy of www.iStockphoto.com

iStock_000000213548 (Dodge Viper GTS ACR - 2000 by Stan Rohrer)

PERFORMANCE TIP

An American flag and Dodge Viper GTS classic car (2000 vintage) are also available on the DVD. The steps to creating a USA classic car and flag are pretty much the same as for the British car. A non-destructive dodge and burn layer was however grouped with the car layer to darken the tires and edge of windshield. Select the color of the car using the Eyedropper tool and paint in Darken mode at 20% in a new layer grouped with the car layer to darken the paint further.

Project 6

Preserving Shadows

The flower for this project was photographed (using a digital compact) on a cold winter's morning in the temperate hills of Victoria, Australia whilst the sand (shot on Kodachrome film) hails from the Great Indian Desert in Rajasthan. Unlikely bedfellows, but with a little craft the two can lie together comfortably within the same frame - but only if the shadow (created by a not-so-subtle 75 watt globe and a couple of pieces of white paper) is captured with all of its subtlety and delicately transplanted to its new home in the desert.

RAW IMAGE ON DVD

The 'shadow catcher' technique - designed to preserve the natural shadows of a subject

Capture your subject against a plain white backdrop. For bigger subjects you just need a bigger backdrop. Professional studio photographers photographing full length models use a curved backdrop that extends from beneath the model's feet to the far wall in one continuous arc. If the white backdrop is to appear white then the backdrop has to be lit as well as the model. The surface should be smooth so the texture of the backdrop is not transplanted along with the shape of the shadow. In this project the white backdrop (a few sheets of printing paper) is separated from the subject using a mask and then placed in the 'Multiply' blend mode to make it invisible. The shadow which is not white blends with the new background.

Botanical Health Warning: The delicate petals of the flower can be cooked, frazzled or fried by the heat of a tungsten lamp in just a few minutes. Be prepared to work quickly or use soft window light as a low-temperature alternative.

1. Place the subject on its own layer above the new background and then duplicate this layer. Add a Levels adjustment layer between the two layers and 'Group' the top layer with this adjustment layer. Create an accurate mask that hides the background of the top layer. Switching off the layer directly above the background may make this task easier.

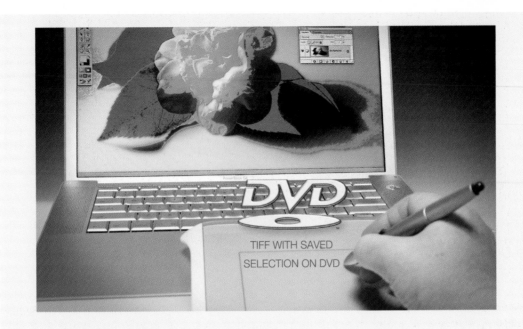

PERFORMANCE TIP

Use any combination of the selection techniques outlined in the previous projects or for really tricky selections consider investing in a Wacom graphics tablet. This allows you to paint using a pen instead of your mouse with the Selection Brush tool.

2. Group a Levels adjustment layer, this time above the Camelia layer. Now move the Highlight slider to the left to clip (or render white) all of the levels that are not part of the shadow on the right side of the image. Ignore the left side of the image for the time being.

PERFORMANCE TIP

Holding down the Alt key as you move the White slider in the Levels dialog box will give you an accurate idea of when the backdrop becomes 255 white.

3. The Levels adjustment that has been applied to the right side of the image will clip some of the delicate shadows on the left side of the image. To restore these delicate shadows you will need to mask this side of the image from this overly aggressive Levels adjustment. Use the Gradient tool with the 'Linear' and 'Black, White' or 'Foreground to Transparent' options (if black is the foreground color) to draw a short gradient in the center of the image from left to right.

4. Create another Levels adjustment layer (grouped with the other adjustment layer) and concentrate on making the left side of the image white whilst leaving the shadows intact. Be careful not to clip the really subtle shadows just beneath the tip of the leaf. When this has been achieved draw a gradient in the opposite direction to prevent the right side of the image being adjusted a second time.

5. A third adjustment layer can be used to render any remaining gray areas of the backdrop white. Fill the adjustment layer with black and then paint with white to clean the backdrop selectively.

6. Any details that cannot be clipped using the Levels adjustment layers can be removed by painting them white on the base layer of the clipping group. Although this is considered destructive editing it should be remembered that this layer has also been duplicated and these pixels could be retrieved if necessary from the top layer.

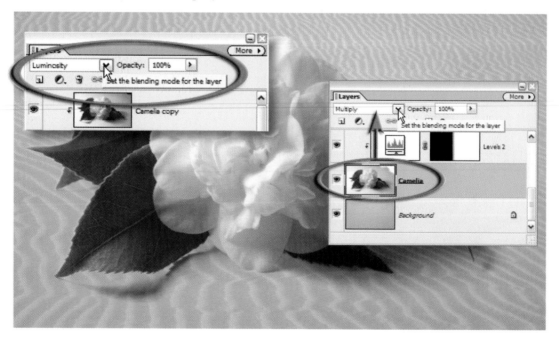

7. Switch the blend mode of all three adjustment layers to 'Luminosity' mode to remove any color that may have been introduced into the shadows and then switch the blend mode of the base layer of the clipping group to 'Multiply' mode. The white will now be rendered transparent whilst the shadows will be blended into the underlying background hue, color and brightness.

8. Use the Minimum/Maximum filters or a Levels adjustment on the layer mask if a white halo is visible around the subject. If a halo is present only in a localized area make a feathered selection around the offending area prior to moving the edge.

9. To complete this project add a Levels adjustment layer above the new background. Move the Gamma slider to the left to brighten the midtones in the background image. Add a Linear gradient (black, white) to the layer mask to shield the foreground from the adjustment. This step gives a little more sense of perspective to the finished result as color and tone fade into the distance.

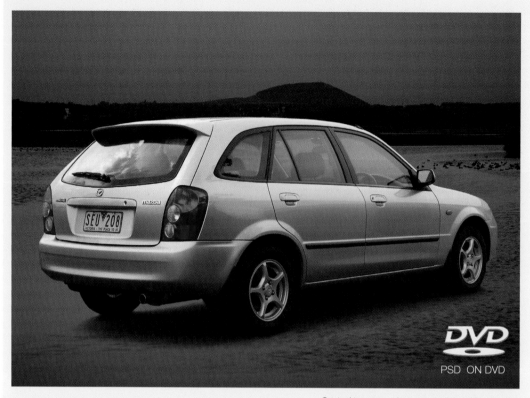

PSD ON DVD

Original images and concept by Jakub Kazmierczak

PERFORMANCE TIP

This technique for preserving shadows does not have to be restricted to small objects sitting on paper. The technique is just as effective when isolating the shadow of a much larger object captured in its natural surroundings. If however the subject has been captured on a textured or rough surface this surface quality will be transferred to the new background when using this technique. A surface quality mismatch can occur that can make the shadow look unnatural.

To ensure a shadow with a rough surface texture does not look out of place against the smooth surface of a new background you can apply a small amount of Gaussian Blur to soften the quality of the shadow. In the illustration on this page a colored Linear gradient in Overlay mode has also been used to warm up the cool colors evident in the panels of the car. The detail in the car windows has also been softened using a Gaussian Blur. These measures ensure the car is perfectly at home in its new surroundings - even if it is balancing on water!

PSD ON DVD

PERFORMANCE TIP

If it is not possible to preserve the original shadow, try to capture a second image from the direction of the light source. This second image will allow you to create a more accurate shadow than simply using the outline of the subject as seen from the camera angle instead of the direction of the light source. Start this technique by making a mask of your subject and place it on a layer above a new background you wish to use. Import the second image captured from the direction of the light source and position it between the subject layer and the background layer. Make a selection of the subject in this second image (your shadow resource), create a new empty layer that sits below the actual subject and above the background layer, and then fill this selection with black. You can then hide or delete the layer that the selection was made from. Place your new shadow layer in Multiply mode. Lower the opacity of your shadow layer and apply the Gaussian Blur filter. Use the Free Transform command to distort and move the shadow into position.

Project 7

Panoramas

Explore the advanced techniques for stitching images that Adobe's Photomerge refuses to stitch seamlessly. Although Photomerge is an excellent tool for the alignment of images it often provides unsatisfactory transitions, especially in skies where the natural vignetting of the camera lens and the short transition zone used by Photomerge makes the visible step in color and tone inevitable.

Spot the joins - upgrade from 6 to 12 megapixels with seamless stitching

Save time in the post-production editing by photographing with a 30-50% overlap, manual exposure and white balance setting (or processed identically using the camera RAW plugin). Although this is not exactly a quick fix, the results can be truly seamless - an excellent way of widening your horizons or turning your 6 megapixel compact into a 12 megapixel blockbuster.

First port of call for stitching images is often Adobe's Photomerge feature. If the results in Photomerge are less than impressive a manual stitch should be considered.

1. The first step in the process is to increase the canvas size (Image > Resize > Canvas Size) to accept the incoming images. When the canvas size has been increased drag in the next image that requires stitching.

2. Switch the second image to Difference mode in the Layers palette and use the Move tool to align the left edge. When the images are aligned on this edge the white lines will be reduced or eliminated.

Note > Unless you use a specialized panoramic tripod head to capture your images you will only be able to align the foreground or background information - not both (this is due to parallax error). In the example above the distant hills are the target alignment point.

3. Choose the Free Transform command (Image > Transform > Free transform or Ctrl+T). Move the reference point location in the Options bar to the left-hand side (the one that you have just aligned). Highlight (double-click) the figures in the Rotation field in the Options bar and then use the up and down arrow keys on the keyboard to rotate the image to achieve alignment.

4. When alignment has been achieved with the first pair of images return the blend mode of the top layer to 'Normal'. Then repeat the first three steps to add additional images to the panorama. When all images are in place use the new Straighten tool to perfect the final rotation of the image. Users of Elements 3.0 can proceed straight to step 4 and rotate the crop marquee to achieve perfect alignment.

Note > Consider locking the layers that you have aligned to stop them being moved inadvertently.

5. Select the 'Crop tool' in the Tools palette and choose the 'No Restriction' option in the Options bar. Drag the crop marquee over the image to remove all of the white canvas background, leaving only the image. Hit the Enter key or double-click inside the crop marquee to complete the crop.

6. Select the 'Magic Wand tool' from the Tools palette and choose the 'Add to selection', 'Contiguous', and 'Sample All Layers' options. Create a selection of the sky by clicking as many times as required. If the selection invades the foreground area lower the 'Tolerance' and repeat the process. Feather the selection by 1 or 2 pixels (Select > Feather) and then save your selection (Select > Save Selection) for use in the merging process later. Now choose 'Deselect' from the Select menu.

PERFORMANCE TIP
Even if the white balance and exposure were identical for the images to be stitched, it is still possible to get small differences in tone or color between a pair of layers. If this is the case, use a Levels adjustment layer to create a closer match between the two. When working above the background layer you will need to group the Levels adjustment layer to prevent the adjustment flowing down to all of the layers underneath the target layer.

PERFORMANCE TIP

One of the problems contributing to the difficulty of obtaining a seamless stitch in the sky is a small amount of vignetting in the corners of the image. This darkening is even more obvious when placed in the center of the adjoining image. This problem can be eased by trimming off a small amount of the edge. First make a selection using the rectangular Marquee tool and then use the Backspace key to remove the selected pixels. Be careful not to place the new edge through significant detail that could also lead to problems in the stitching process.

7. Prepare for the stitching process by creating a Levels adjustment layer (no adjustment required) directly below the second image. Group the second image to this Levels adjustment layer. Double-click the background layer and click OK when the New Layer dialog box opens. This will allow you to lower the opacity of this layer, which in turn will help in the merging process. Create a new layer, fill with white and drag this new layer to the bottom of the layers stack. Then go to the Select menu and choose 'Load Selection'. Load your selection of the sky and check the Invert box.

rise_finish.psd @ 25% (Levels 2, Layer Mask/8)

8. Make sure that black is the foreground color and then choose the 'Brush tool'. Select a large soft edged brush and set the opacity to 100%. Make sure the layer mask that is at the base of the clipping group is selected and then, whilst holding down the Shift key to constrain the brush stroke, click at the top and the bottom of the edge to be merged.

9. If you targeted the alignment in steps 2 and 3 on the background hills, then the foreground detail will not be 100% aligned. This will be apparent in the region of the brush stroke that you have just made, especially where there are strong graphic lines present that create the illusion of a 'ghost image'. Select 'White' as the foreground color, reduce the size of the brush and then paint into the mask to remove the most obvious aspects of this ghost image.

10. Invert the selection (Select > Inverse) and then choose the 'Gradient tool'. Choose either the 'Foreground (Black) to Transparent' gradient or the 'Black, White' gradient in 'Multiply' mode to ensure your second gradient does not remove the previous brush stroke. Lowering the opacity of the top layer will reveal the overlap between the two images. Drag your gradient the length of this overlap to ensure a slow transition. This slow transition in the sky will ensure the tell-tale banding that often results with Photomerge will not be evident. Now repeat the process for adding additional images until the merging process is complete.

11. When the merging process is complete the image enhancement can start. Consider working the tonality or color, adding some gradients and last, but not least, the Unsharp Mask layer.

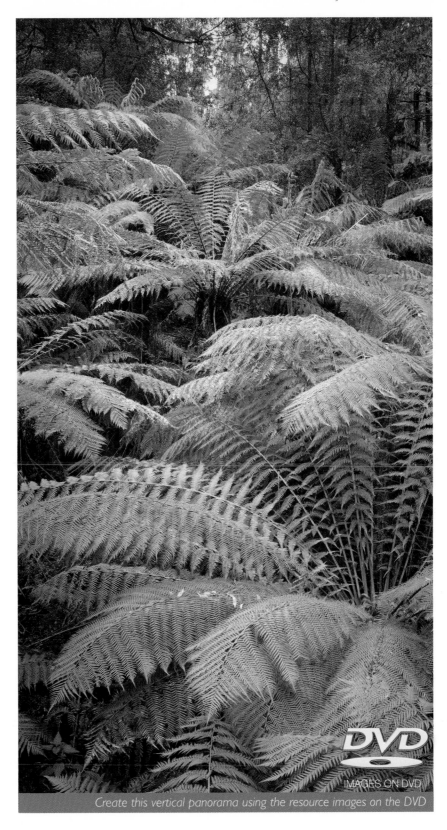

Create this vertical panorama using the resource images on the DVD

Project 8

Photograph by Daniel Stainsby

Use the Mask Hair Against White
action to fast-track this technique

Hair Transplant

One of the most challenging montage or masking jobs in the profession of post-production editing is the hair lift. When the model has long flowing hair and the subject needs to change location many post-production artists call in sick. Get it wrong and, just like a bad wig, it shows. Extract filters, Magic Erasers and Tragic Extractors don't even get us close. The first secret step must be completed before you even press the shutter on the camera. Your number one essential step for success is to first shoot your model against a white backdrop, sufficiently illuminated so that it is captured as white rather than gray. This important aspect of the initial image capture ensures that the resulting hair transplant is seamless and undetectable. The post-production is the easy bit - simply apply the correct sequence of editing steps and the magic is all yours. This is not brain surgery but follow these simple steps and you will join the elite ranks of Photoshop gurus around the world. Celebrity status is just a few clicks away.

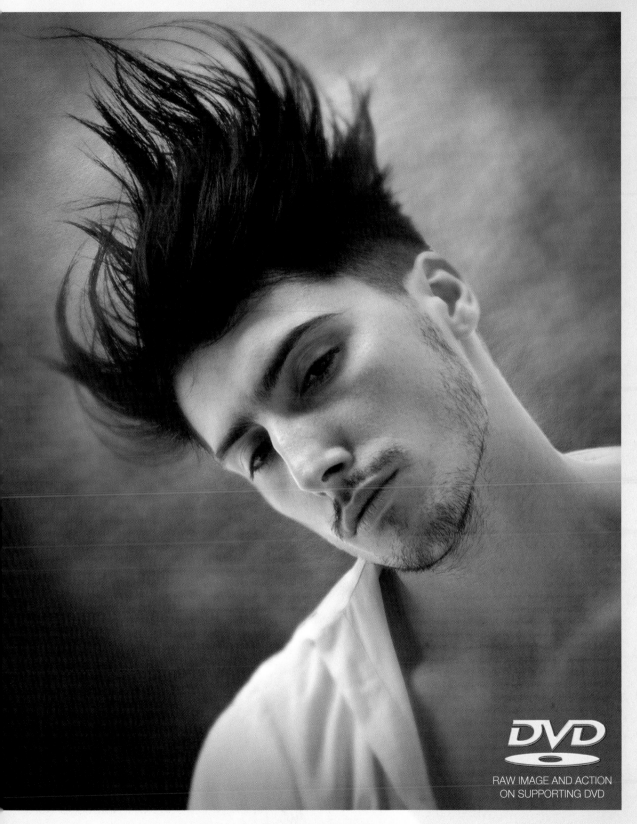

RAW IMAGE AND ACTION
ON SUPPORTING DVD

Hair extraction – not as painful as pulling teeth

Stage 1: Masking hair - tips for tremendous transplants

1. The initial steps of this tutorial are concerned with creating a mask that can be used in the final montage. Start by dragging the background layer to the New Layer icon to duplicate it. Choose 'Remove Color' from the Adjust Color submenu found in the Enhance menu (Enhance > Adjust Color > Remove Color). Drag this desaturated/monochrome layer to the New Layer icon in the Layers palette to duplicate it. Set the blend mode of this new layer (now on top of the layers stack) to 'Overlay' mode.

2. From the Layer menu choose 'Merge Down' to create a single high-contrast monochrome layer. Select 'Black' as the foreground color and the 'Brush tool' from the Tools palette. Choose a large hard edged brush and 100% opacity from the Options bar and set the mode to 'Overlay' (also in the Options bar). Painting in Overlay mode will preserve the white background and darken the rest of the pixels. Accuracy whilst painting in Overlay mode is not a concern when the background is white or is significantly lighter than the subject. Avoid going anywhere near the tips of the hair at this stage.

3. Even the bright tones of the white shirt can be rendered black by repeatedly clicking the mouse whilst using a large brush in Overlay mode. Again it is important to avoid going anywhere near the hair.

4. Darken the body of the hair near the scalp but avoid the locks of hair that have white background showing through. Painting these individual strands of hair will thicken the hair and may lead to subsequent halos appearing later in the montage process.

PERFORMANCE TIP

Switch the blend mode of the brush in the Options bar to 'Normal' mode when painting away from the edge of the subject. This will ensure a speedy conclusion to the mask making process. The mask is now ready to use in the montage.

Note > If any of the background has been darkened in the process of creating a black and white mask switch the foreground color to 'White' and choose 'Overlay' in the Options bar. Paint to render any areas of gray background white. It is again important to avoid painting near the edges containing delicate hair detail.

5. With the Remove Color layer selected add a Levels adjustment layer. Without making any adjustment simply select OK. This Levels adjustment layer has a layer mask that we can use to house the mask that we have created in the previous step.

6. The next step relocates the mask you have just created into the layer mask of the adjustment layer. From the Select menu choose 'All' and from the Edit menu choose 'Copy Merged'. Hold down the Alt key and click on the layer mask thumbnail in the Layers palette. The image window will momentarily appear white as you view the empty contents of the layer mask. From the Edit menu choose 'Paste' to transfer the contents of the clipboard to this layer mask. Click on the layer below to select it and then click on the Visibility icon of this layer to switch it off. This mask layer serves no purpose now that it has been successfully transferred to the adjustment layer mask.

7. The new background is placed on its own layer above the figure and mask layers. Drag the thumbnail of this new file into the image window of your project file from either the Photo Bin or the layer thumbnail in the Layers palette. Group this new background layer with the adjustment layer beneath (Layer > Group with Previous). Alternatively you can hold down the Alt key and click on the dividing line between the two layers to group them.

8. Grouping the new background with the adjustment layer will mask the background in the region of the figure but the quality will not yet be acceptable. Setting the blend mode of the adjustment layer to 'Multiply' will bring back all of the fine detail in the hair. The background will be not darkened by applying the 'Multiply' blend mode as white is a neutral color. The subtle detail in the fine strands of hair will however be preserved in all their glory.

9. The accuracy and quality of the edge of the mask will usually require some attention in order for the subject to achieve a seamless quality with the new background. Make a selection of all of the edges that do not include any hair detail using the Lasso tool with a small amount of feather set in the Options bar. With the adjustment layer mask selected choose the 'Gaussian Blur filter' (Filter > Blur > Gaussian Blur) and apply a 1- to 2-pixel Radius Blur to the mask. Click OK and then from the Enhance menu choose a Levels adjustment from the Adjust lighting submenu. Move the central Gamma slider underneath the histogram to realign the edge of the mask with the subject edge (no dark or light halo should be visible).

PERFORMANCE TIP

If the mask is too soft the edges can be sharpened by moving the black and white sliders in towards the central Gamma slider a little. Select OK when perfect alignment has been achieved.
Zoom in to 100% Actual pixels whilst working to accurately assess the quality of your mask.

10. In most instances the hair is already looking pretty fabulous but to modify and perfect the hair even further you will need to inverse the selection (Select > Inverse). Choose 'Levels' once again and move the central Gamma slider to the left to increase the density of the hair and eliminate any white halos that may be present. Moving the White slider to the left a little may help the process of achieving a perfect blend between subject and background. Select OK and choose 'Deselect' from the Select menu.

PERFORMANCE TIP

Any localized refinement of the mask can be achieved manually by painting with a small soft edged brush directly into the layer mask. Paint with white at a reduced opacity (10-20%) to remove any fine halos present in localized areas. Several brush strokes will slowly erase the halo from the image.

11. The true test of an accurate mask for a subject that was photographed against a white background is when you place the subject against a very dark background. Grouping a Levels adjustment layer with the new background layer can darken the background image used in this project. Hold down the Alt key when you select a Levels adjustment layer from the Layers palette. Click on the Group with Previous box in the New Layer dialog box and then select OK to open the Levels dialog box. Move the Gamma slider to the right in order to preview your subject against a darker background in the image window.

Stage 2: Split tone styling and depth of field tweaking

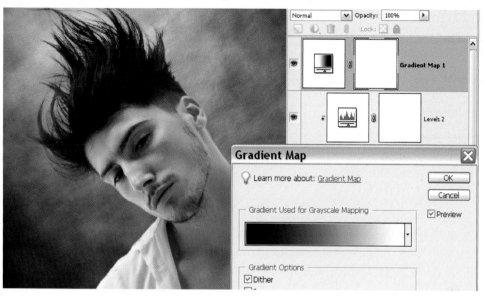

12. Now that the hair transplant is complete the styling can commence. Select the top layer in the Layers palette and then click on the Create Adjustment Layer icon and choose 'Gradient Map'. I have applied one of the split tone presets that is available on the supporting DVD. See the toning project in Part 2 of this book. A split tone that has a cool shadow tone and warm highlight tone has been used to achieve the split tone effect for this project.

13. A shallow depth of field can be achieved by first merging the contents of all of the layers to a new layer. With the top layer in the Layers palette selected choose 'All' from the Select menu and then choose 'Copy Merged' from the Edit menu. Click on the New Layer icon in the Layers palette and then choose 'Paste' from the Edit menu. The keyboard shortcut for the last sequence of commands is to hold down the Ctrl, Shift and Alt keys whilst pressing the letter E on the keyboard (users of Elements 3.0 must type the letter N followed by the letter E). Apply a 4-pixel Gaussian Blur to this layer (Filter > Blur > Gaussian Blur).

14. Click on the layer beneath the merged layer (the one you have just blurred) and then create a Levels adjustment layer. Select OK without making any adjustment. Group the layer above with this adjustment layer and then click on the adjustment layer mask to select it. Select the 'Gradient tool' from the Tools palette and choose 'Reflected Gradient' and the 'Black, White' options from the Options bar. Click in the central part of the model's face and drag outwards to a position just beyond the ear. The sharp focus should now be restored to the central portion of the face only.

15. Create a vignette for this image. In this project I have created a new layer that has been filled with white and set to Multiply mode (hold down the Alt key as you click on the New Layer icon to access all of these options). A selection is then made using the Elliptical Marquee tool, feathered by 100 pixels (Select > Feather) and then in the Fill Layer dialog box, in the Contents section, choose 'Use Black' (Edit > Fill Selection). The vignette is then subdued by lowering the opacity of the layer.

Note > A small amount of noise must be added if you are creating a vignette in a very smooth-toned background in order to prevent any tonal banding (Filter > Noise > Add Noise).

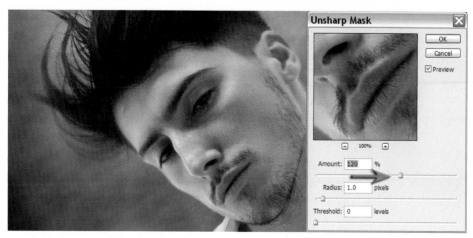

16. Create a merged copy of all of the layers (hold down the Ctrl+Shift+Alt keys and type the letter E as in step 14) and apply the Unsharp Mask (Enhance > Unsharp Mask) to complete the project.

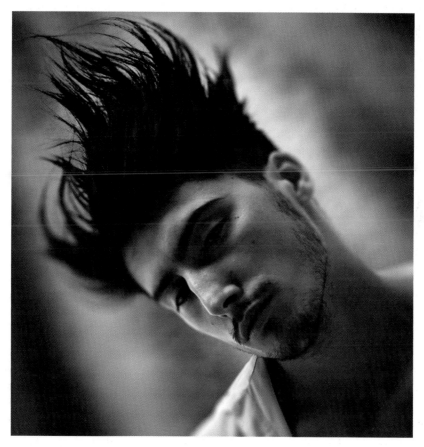

To change the scenery (background) simply trash the sharpened and blurred layers and cut and paste a new image into the layer that was clipped with your adjustment layer mask. One face, lots of hair – a million locations. Now you don't have to put a hat on to go traveling.

MAXIMUM PERFORMANCE

When masking hair that was shot against a black background setting the Levels adjustment layer (the one holding the mask) to the Screen Blend mode is the secret to success. Note the difference between Normal mode and Screen Blend mode in the illustrations above.

You will need to invert the layer mask when using a model shot against a black background (Filter > Adjustments > Invert). Paint in Overlay mode as in steps 2 to 4 of the Hair Transplant project. Apply a Levels adjustment to the layer mask and fine-tune the brightness of the hair against the background by moving the Gamma slider (see the Performance Tip on page 255).

Maximum Performance

Use the Mask Hair Against Black
action to fast-track this technique

DVD
IMAGES ON DVD

image courtesy of www.iStockphoto.com   Create this portrait using the resource images on the DVD

Jargon Buster

A

Adjustment layers: *Non-destructive (always editable) image adjustment placed on a layer.*

Adobe gamma: *A calibration and profiling utility supplied with Photoshop.*

Aliasing: *The display of a digital image where a diagonal or curved line appears jagged due to the square pixels.*

Anti-aliasing: *The process of smoothing the appearance of lines in a digital image.*

Artifacts: *Pixels that are significantly incorrect in their brightness or color values.*

B

Bit: *Short for binary digit, the basic unit of the binary language.*

Bit depth: *Number of bits (memory) assigned to recording color or tonal information.*

Blend mode: *The formula used for defining the mixing of a layer with those beneath it.*

Brightness: *The value assigned to a pixel in the HSB model to define the relative lightness of a pixel.*

Byte: *Eight bits. Standard unit of data storage containing a value between 0 and 255.*

C

CCD: *Charge coupled device. A solid state sensor used in digital image capture.*

Channel: *A division of color or luminance data.*

Clipboard: *The temporary storage of something that has been cut or copied.*

Clipping group: *Two or more layers that have been linked. The base layer acts as a mask limiting the effect or visibility of those layers clipped to it.*

Cloning tool: *A tool used for replicating pixels.*

Color fringing: *Bands of color on the edges of lines within an image.*

Color gamut: *The range of colors provided by a hardware device, or a set of pigments.*

Color management: *A system to ensure uniformity of color between the subject, monitor display and final print.*

Color Picker: *Dialog box used for the selection of colors.*

Compression: *A method for reducing the file size of a digital image.*

Constrain proportions: *Retain the proportional dimensions of an image when changing the image size.*

Continuous tone: *An image containing the illusion of smooth gradations between highlights and shadows.*

Contrast: *The difference in brightness between the darkest and lightest areas of the image or subject.*

Crash: *The sudden operational failure of a computer.*

Crop: *Reduce image size to enhance composition or limit information.*

Curves: *A control in the full version of Adobe Photoshop only for adjusting tonality and color.*

D

Default: A 'normal' or 'start' setting as chosen by the manufacturer or user.

Depth of field: The zone of sharpness variable by aperture, focal length or subject distance.

Download: To copy digital files (usually from the Internet).

Dpi: Dots per inch. A measurement of resolution.

E

Editable text: Text that has not been rendered into pixels.

Exposure: Combined effect of intensity and duration of light on a light sensitive material or image sensor.

Exposure compensation: To increase or decrease the exposure from a meter-indicated exposure to obtain an appropriate exposure.

F

Feather: The action of softening the edge of a digital selection.

File format: The code used to store digital data, e.g. TIFF or JPEG.

File size: The memory required to store digital data in a file.

Format: The orientation or shape of the image or the erasure of a memory device.

Freeze: Software that fails to interact with new information.

G

Galleries: A managed collection of images displayed in a conveniently accessible form.

Gaussian Blur: A filter used for defocussing a digital image.

Gigabyte: A unit of measurement for digital files, 1024 megabytes.

Grayscale: An 8-bit image used to describe monochrome (black and white) images.

H

High Dynamic Range (HDR): A subject brightness range that exceeds the ability of the capture medium (film or sensor) to record both the highlight and shadow information simultaneously.

Highlight: Area of subject receiving highest exposure value.

Histogram: A graphical representation of a digital image indicating the pixels allocated to each level.

Hue: The name of a color, e.g. red or green.

I

Image size: The pixel dimensions, output dimensions and resolution used to define a digital image.

Interpolation: Increasing the pixel dimensions of an image by inserting new pixels between existing pixels within the image.

ISO: International Standards Organization. A numerical system for rating the speed or relative light sensitivity of a film or sensor.

J

JPEG (.jpg): Joint Photographic Experts Group. Popular but lossy (i.e. destructive) image compression file format.

K

Kilobyte: 1024 bytes.

L

Lasso tool: Selection tool used in digital editing.

Latitude: Ability of the film or device to record the brightness range of the subject.

Layer mask: A mask attached to an adjustment layer that is used to define the visibility of the adjustment. It can also be used to limit the visibility of pixels on the layer above if that layer is grouped or clipped with the adjustment layer.

Layers: A feature in digital editing software that allows a composite digital image where each element is on a separate layer or level.

Levels: Shades of lightness or brightness assigned to pixels.

LZW compression: Lossless compression that may be used in the TIFF format.

M

Magic Wand tool: Selection tool used in digital editing.

Marching ants: A moving broken line indicating a digital selection of pixels.

Marquee tool: Selection tool used in digital editing.

Megabyte: A unit of measurement for digital files, 1024 kilobytes.

Megapixels: More than a million pixels.

Memory card: A removable storage device about the size of a small card.

Minimum aperture: Smallest lens opening.

Mode (digital image): The tonal and color range of the captured or scanned image.

N

Noise: Electronic interference producing speckles in the image.

O

Opacity: The degree of non-transparency.

Opaque: Not transmitting light.

Optimize: The process of fine-tuning the file size and display quality of an image.

Out of gamut: Beyond the scope of colors that a particular device can create, reproduce or display.

P

Pixel: The smallest square picture element in a digital image.

Pixellated: An image where the pixels are visible to the human eye and curved or diagonal lines appear jagged or stepped.

Primary colors: The three colors of light (red, green and blue).

R

RAM: *Random access memory. The computer's short-term or working memory.*

Reflector: *A surface used to reflect light in order to fill shadows.*

Resample: *To alter the total number of pixels describing a digital image.*

Resolution: *A measure of the degree of definition, also called 'sharpness'.*

RGB: *Red, green and blue. The three primary colors used to display images on a color monitor.*

Rubber Stamp: *Another name for the Clone Stamp tool used for replicating pixels.*

S

Sample: *To select a color value for analysis or use.*

Saturation (color): *Intensity or richness of color hue.*

Save As: *An option that allows the user to create a duplicate of a digital file with an alternative name or in a different location.*

Scale: *A ratio of size.*

Scratch disk: *Portion of hard disk allocated to software such as Elements to be used as a working space.*

Screen redraws: *Time taken to render information being depicted on the monitor as changes are being made through the application software.*

Sharp: *In focus. Not blurred.*

Sliders: *A sliding control to adjust settings such as color, tone, opacity, etc.*

Stamp Visible: *The action of copying the visible elements from a number of layers and pasting them on to a new layer.*

System software: *Computer operating program, e.g. Windows or Mac OS.*

T

TIFF: *Tagged Image File Format. Popular image file format for desktop publishing applications.*

Tone: *A tint of color or shade of gray.*

Transparent: *Allowing light to pass through.*

U

Unsharp Mask: *See USM.*

USM: *Unsharp Mask. A filter used to sharpen images.*

W

Workflow: *Series of repeatable steps required to achieve a particular result within a digital imaging environment.*

Z

Zoom tool: *A tool used for magnifying a digital image on the monitor.*

Shortcuts

 Printable PDF file on DVD

Action   Keyboard Shortcut

Navigate and view

Action	Keyboard Shortcut
Fit image on screen	Ctrl+0
View image at 100% (actual pixels)	Alt+Ctrl+0
Zoom tool (magnify)	Ctrl+Spacebar+click image or Ctrl++
Zoom tool (reduce)	Alt+Spacebar+click image or Ctrl+-
Show/hide rulers	Shift+Ctrl+R
Hide palettes	Tab key

File commands

Action	Keyboard Shortcut
Open	Ctrl+O
Close	Ctrl+W
Save	Ctrl+S
Save As	Ctrl+Shift+S
Undo	Ctrl+Z
Redo	Ctrl+Y

Selections

Action	Keyboard Shortcut
Add to selection	Hold Shift key and select again
Subtract from selection	Hold Alt key and select again
Copy	Ctrl+C
Cut	Ctrl+X
Paste	Ctrl+V
Paste into selection	Ctrl+Shift+V
Free Transform	Ctrl+T
Distort image in Free Transform	Hold Ctrl Key+move handle
Feather	Alt+Ctrl+D
Select All	Ctrl+A
Deselect	Ctrl+D
Reselect	Shift+Ctrl+D
Inverse selection	Shift+Ctrl+I

Painting

Set default foreground and background colors	D
Switch between foreground and background colors	X
Enlarge brush size (with Paint tool selected)	]
Reduce brush size (with Paint tool selected)	[
Make brush softer	[+Shift
Make brush harder	]+Shift
Change opacity of brush in 10% increments (with Paint tool selected)	Press number keys 0-9
Fill with foreground color	Alt+Backspace
Fill with background color	Ctrl+Backspace

Image adjustments

Levels	Ctrl+L
Hue/Saturation	Ctrl+U
Group layer	Ctrl+G

Layers and masks

Add new layer	Shift+Ctrl+N
Load selection from layer mask	Ctrl+click thumbnail
Change opacity of active layer in 10% increments	Press number keys 0-9
Add layer mask - Hide All	Alt+click Add Layer Mask icon
Move layer down/up	Ctrl+[or]
Stamp Visible	Ctrl+Alt+Shift then type E
Disable/enable layer mask	Shift+click layer mask thumbnail
View layer mask only	Alt+click layer mask thumbnail
View layer mask and image	Alt+Shift+ click layer mask thumbnail
Blend modes	Alt+Shift+(F, N, S, M, O, Y) Soft Light, Normal, Screen, Multiply, Overlay, Luminosity

Crop

Enter crop	Enter key
Cancel crop	Esc key
Constrain proportions of crop marquee	Hold Shift key
Turn off magnetic guides when cropping	Hold Alt+Shift keys+drag handle

Index